CliffsNotes™

The Scarlet Letter

By Susan Van Kirk, M.A.

IN THIS BOOK

- Learn about the Life and Background of the Author
- Preview an Introduction to the Novel
- Explore themes, literary devices, and character development in the Critical Commentaries
- Examine in-depth Character Analyses
- Reinforce what you learn with CliffsNotes Review
- Find additional information to further your study in CliffsNotes Resource Center and online at www.cliffsnotes.com

Hungry Minds™

Best-Selling Books • Digital Downloads • e-Books • Answer Networks • e-Newsletters • Branded Web Sites • e-Learning

New York, NY • Cleveland, OH • Indianapolis, IN

About the Author

Susan Van Kirk has taught high school English in Monmouth, Illinois, for 30 years.

Publisher's Acknowledgments

Editorial

Project Editor: Tracy Barr

Acquisitions Editor: Greg Tubach

Editorial Assistant: Michelle Hacker

Glossary Editors: Webster's New World Dictionaries

Acquisitions Editor: Greg Tubach

Production

Indexer: York Production Services, Inc.

Proofreader: York Production Services, Inc.

CliffsNotes *The Scarlet Letter*

Published by:

Hungry Minds, Inc.

909 Third Avenue

New York, NY 10022

www.hungryminds.com

www.cliffsnotes.com (CliffsNotes Web site)

ISBN: 0-7645-8605-X

Printed in the United States of America

10 9 8 7 6 5 4 3

1O/SY/QZ/QR/IN

Distributed in the United States by Hungry Minds, Inc.

Distributed by CDG Books Canada Inc. for Canada; by Transworld Publishers Limited in the United Kingdom; by IDG Norge Books for Norway; by IDG Sweden Books for Sweden; by IDG Books Australia Publishing Corporation Pty. Ltd. for Australia and New Zealand; by TransQuest Publishers Pte Ltd. for Singapore, Malaysia, Thailand, Indonesia, and Hong Kong; by Gotop Information Inc. for Taiwan; by ICG Muse, Inc. for Japan; by Norma Comunicaciones S.A. for Columbia; by Intersoft for South Africa; by Eyrolles for France; by International Thomson Publishing for Germany, Austria and Switzerland; by Distribuidora Cuspide for Argentina; by LR International for Brazil; by Galileo Libros for Chile; by Ediciones ZETA S.C.R. Ltda. for Peru; by WS Computer Publishing Corporation, Inc., for the Philippines; by Contemporanea de Ediciones for Venezuela; by Express Computer Distributors for the Caribbean and West Indies; by Micronesia Media Distributor, Inc. for Micronesia; by Grupo Editorial Norma S.A. for Guatemala; by Chips Computadoras S.A. de C.V. for Mexico; by Editorial Norma de Panama S.A. for Panama; by American Bookshops for Finland. Authorized Sales Agent: Anthony Rudkin Associates for the Middle East and North Africa.

For general information on Hungry Minds' products and services please contact our Customer Care department; within the U.S. at 800-762-2974, outside the U.S. at 317-572-3993 or fax 317-572-4002.

For sales inquiries and resellers information, including discounts, premium and bulk quantity sales and foreign language translations please contact our Customer Care department at 800-434-3422, fax 317-572-4002 or write to Hungry Minds, Inc., Attn: Customer Care department, 10475 Crosspoint Boulevard, Indianapolis, IN 46256.

For information on licensing foreign or domestic rights, please contact our Sub-Rights Customer Care department at 212-884-5000.

For information on using Hungry Minds' products and services in the classroom or for ordering examination copies, please contact our Educational Sales department at 800-434-2086 or fax 317-572-4005.

Please contact our Public Relations department at 212-884-5163 for press review copies or 212-884-5000 for author interviews and other publicity information or fax 212-884-5400.

For authorization to photocopy items for corporate, personal, or educational use, please contact Copyright Clearance Center, 222 Rosewood Drive, Danvers, MA 01923, or fax 978-750-4470.

Library of Congress Cataloging-in-Publication Data

Van Kirk, Susan, 1946-

CliffsNotes *The Scarlet Letter* / by Susan Van Kirk.

p. cm.

Includes bibliographical references and index.

ISBN 0-7645-8605-X (alk. paper)

1. Hawthorne, Nathaniel, 1804-1864. Scarlet letter--Examinations--Study guides. I. Title: On Hawthorne's The scarlet letter. II. Title.

PS1868.V36 2000

813'.3--dc21

00--035105

CIP

Hungry Minds˜is a trademark of Hungry Minds, Inc.

Table of Contents

How to Use This Book

CliffsNotes *The Scarlet Letter* supplements the original work, giving you background information about the author, an introduction to the novel, a graphical character map, critical commentaries, expanded glossaries, and a comprehensive index. CliffsNotes Review tests your comprehension of the original text and reinforces learning with questions and answers, practice projects, and more. For further information on Nathaniel Hawthorne and *The Scarlet Letter,* check out the CliffsNotes Resource Center.

CliffsNotes provides the following icons to highlight essential elements of particular interest:

Reveals the underlying themes in the work.

Helps you to more easily relate to or discover the depth of a character.

Uncovers elements such as setting, atmosphere, mystery, passion, violence, irony, symbolism, tragedy, foreshadowing, and satire.

Enables you to appreciate the nuances of words and phrases.

Don't Miss Our Web Site

Discover classic literature as well as modern-day treasures by visiting the CliffsNotes Web site at www.cliffsnotes.com. You can obtain a quick download of a CliffsNotes title, purchase a title in print form, browse our catalog, or view online samples.

You'll also find interactive tools that are fun and informative, links to interesting Web sites, tips, articles, and additional resources to help you, not only for literature, but for test prep, finance, careers, computers, and Internet too. See you at www.cliffsnotes.com!

LIFE AND BACKGROUND OF THE AUTHOR

Early/Formative Years

Born July 4, 1804, Nathaniel Hathorne was the only son of Captain Nathaniel Hathorne and Elizabeth Clarke Manning Hathorne. (Hawthorne added the "w" to his name after he graduated from college.) Following the death of Captain Hathorne in 1808, Nathaniel, his mother, and his two sisters were forced to move in with Mrs. Hathorne's relatives, the Mannings. Here Nathaniel Hawthorn grew up in the company of women without a strong male role model; this environment may account for what biographers call his shyness and introverted personality.

This period of Hawthorne's life was mixed with the joys of reading and the resentment of financial dependence. While he studied at an early age with Joseph E. Worcester, a well-known lexicographer, he was not particularly fond of school. An injury allowed him to stay home for a year when he was nine, and his early "friends" were books by Shakespeare, Spenser, Bunyan, and 18th century novelists.

During this time Mrs. Hathorne moved her family to land owned by the Mannings near Raymond, Maine. Nathaniel's fondest memories of these days were when "I ran quite wild, and would, I doubt not, have willingly run wild till this time, fishing all day long, or shooting with an old fowling piece." This idyllic life in the wilderness exerted its charm on the boy's imagination but ended in 1819 when he returned to Salem to prepare two years for college entrance.

Education

In 1821, Hawthorne entered Bowdoin College in Brunswick, Maine. Among his classmates were Henry Wadsworth Longfellow, who would become a distinguished poet and Harvard professor, and Franklin Pierce, future 14th president of the United States. Another classmate, Horatio Bridge, was later to offer a Boston publisher a guarantee against loss if he would publish Hawthorne's first collection of short stories.

Hawthorne graduated middle of his class in 1825. Regarding his aspirations, he wrote, "I do not want to be a doctor and live by men's diseases, nor a minister to live by their sins, nor a lawyer to live by their quarrels. So, I don't see that there is anything left for me but to be an author."

Early Career

For the next 12 years, Hawthorne lived in comparative isolation in an upstairs chamber at his mother's house, where he worked at perfecting his writing craft. He also began keeping notebooks or journals, a habit he continued throughout his life. He often jotted down ideas and descriptions, and his words are now a rich source of information about his themes, ideas, style experiments, and subjects.

In 1828, he published his first novel, *Fanshaw: A Tale*, at his own expense. *Fanshaw* was a short, imitation Gothic novel and poorly written. Dissatisfied with this novel, Hawthorne attempted to buy up all the copies so that no one could read it. He did not publish another novel for almost 25 years. By 1838, he had written two-thirds of the short stories he was to write in his lifetime. None of these stories gained him much attention, and he could not interest a publisher in printing a collection of his tales until 1837, when his college friend Horatio Bridge backed the publishing of *Twice-Told Tales,* a collection of Hawthorne's stories that had been published separately in magazines. His schoolmate and friend, Longfellow, reviewed the book with glowing terms. Edgar Allan Poe, known for his excoriating reviews of writers, not only wrote warmly of Hawthorne's book but also took the opportunity to define the short story in his now famous review. *Twice-Told Tales* is considered a masterpiece of literature, and it contains unmistakably American stories.

Financial Burdens and Marriage

In 1838, Hawthorne met Sophia Amelia Peabody, and the following year they were engaged. It was at this time that Hawthorne invested a thousand dollars of his meager capital in the Brook Farm Community at West Roxbury. There he became acquainted with Ralph Waldo Emerson and the naturalist Henry David Thoreau. These transcendentalist thinkers influenced much of Hawthorne's thinking about the importance of intuition rather than intellect in uncovering the truths of nature and human beings. Hawthorne left this experiment in November 1841, disillusioned with the viewpoint of the community, exhausted from the work, and without financial hope that he could support a wife. From this experience, however, he gained the setting for a later novel, *The Blithedale Romance.*

In a trip to Boston after leaving Brook Farm, Hawthorne reached an understanding about a salary for future contributions to the *Democratic Review.* He and Sophia married in Boston on July 9, 1842, and left for Concord, Massachusetts, where they took up residence in the now-famous "Old Manse."

New Challenges and Writings

Hawthorne's life at the "Old Manse" was happy and productive, and these were some of the happiest years of his life. He was newly married, in love with his wife, and surrounded by many of the leading literary figures of the day: Ralph Waldo Emerson, Henry David Thoreau, Margaret Fuller, and Bronson Alcott. During this time, Hawthorne wrote for the *Democratic Review* and produced some tales that would be published in 1846 in *Mosses from an Old Manse.*

Financial problems continued to plague the family, however. The birth of their first child, Una, caused Hawthorne to once again seek a financially secure job. With the help of his old friends, Hawthorne was appointed a surveyor for the port of Salem. His son, Julian, was born in 1846. Although the new job eased the financial problems for the family, Hawthorne again found little time to pursue his writing. Nevertheless, during this time, he was already forming ideas for a novel based on his Puritan ancestry and introduced by a preface about the Custom House where he worked. When the Whigs won the 1848 election, Hawthorne lost his position. It was a financial shock to the family, but it fortuitously provided him with time to write *The Scarlet Letter.*

The Golden Years of Writing

During these years Hawthorne was to write some of the greatest prose of his life. In 1849, Hawthorne wrote *The Scarlet Letter,* which won him much fame and greatly increased his reputation. While warmly received here and abroad, *The Scarlet Letter* sold only 8,000 copies in Hawthorne's lifetime.

In 1849, when the family moved to Lennox, Massachusetts, Hawthorne made the acquaintance of Herman Melville, a young writer who became a good friend. Hawthorne encouraged the young Melville, who later thanked him by dedicating his book, *Moby Dick,* to him. During this—the "Little Red House" period in Lennox—Hawthorne wrote *The House of the Seven Gables* and some minor works that were published in 1851.

Around the time that Nathaniel and Sophia's second daughter, Rose, was born, the family moved to West Newton, where Hawthorne finished and published his novel about the Brook Farm experience, *The Blithedale Romance,* and also *A Wonder Book for Girls and Boys.* Because there was little to no literature published for children, Hawthorne's book was unique in this area.

Later Writing and Years Abroad

In Concord, the Hawthornes found a permanent house, along with nine acres of land, which they purchased from Bronson Alcott, the transcendentalist writer and father of Louisa May Alcott. Hawthorne renamed the house The Wayside, and in May, 1852, he and his family moved in. Here, Hawthorne was to write only two of his works: *Tanglewood Tales,* another collection designed for young readers, and *A Life of Pierce,* a campaign biography for his old friend from college. As a result of the biography, President Pierce awarded Hawthorne with an appointment as United States consul in Liverpool, England. The Hawthornes spent the next seven years in Europe.

Although Hawthorne wrote no additional fiction while serving as consul, he kept a journal that later served as a source of material for *Our Old Home,* a collection of sketches dealing with English scenery, life, and manners published in 1863. While in Italy, Hawthorne kept a notebook that provided material for his final, complete work of fiction, which was published in England as *Transformation* and, in America, as *The Marble Faun.*

The Autumn of His Life

By the autumn of 1863, Hawthorne was a sick man. In May, 1864, he traveled to New Hampshire with his old classmate Pierce in search of improved health. During this trip, he died in his sleep on May 19, 1864, in Plymouth, New Hampshire. He was buried in the Sleepy Hollow Cemetery at Concord. Widely eulogized as one of America's foremost writers, his fellow authors gathered to show their respect. Among his pallbearers were Longfellow, Holmes, Lowell, and Emerson. Today he rests there with Washington Irving, Emerson, Thoreau, and the Alcotts, as well as his wife, Sophia.

INTRODUCTION TO THE NOVEL

Introduction

"The life of the Custom House lies like a dream behind me . . ..
Soon, likewise, my old native town will loom upon me through the
haze of memory, a mist brooding over and around it; as if it were no
portion of the real earth, but an overgrown village in cloud-land, with
only imaginary inhabitants to people its wooden houses, and walk its
homely lanes, and the unpicturesque prolixity of its main street . . . It
may be, however,—oh, transporting and triumphant thought!—that
the great-grandchildren of the present race may sometimes think kindly
of the scribbler of bygone days . . .."

In the mid-1800s when Nathaniel Hawthorne wrote these words in
the Custom House preface to *The Scarlet Letter,* he could not have imagined the millions of readers a century later who would "think kindly of
the scribbler of bygone days" and continue to make his novel a best-
seller. The mist of imagination that falls over Salem, Massachusetts, in
his description is the same aura that permeates the setting of his novel.
Look for the Boston of 1640 in history books, and you will not find
the magical and Gothic elements that abound in Hawthorne's story.
For the mind of genius has created a Boston that is shrouded in darkness and mystery and surrounded by a forest of sunshine and shadow.
In writing *The Scarlet Letter*, Hawthorne was creating a form of fiction
he called the psychological romance, and woven throughout his novel
are elements of Gothic literature. What he created would later be followed by other romances, but never would they attain the number of
readers or the critical acclaim of *The Scarlet Letter.*

Hawthorne began *The Scarlet Letter* in September, 1849, and finished it, amazingly, in February, 1850. Its publication made his literary
reputation and temporarily eased some of his financial burdens. This
novel was the culmination of Hawthorne's own reading, study, and
experimentation with themes about the subjects of Puritans, sin, guilt,
and the human conflict between emotions and intellect. Since its first
publishing in March of 1850, *The Scarlet Letter* has never been out of
print. Even today, Hawthorne's romance is one of the best-selling books
on the market. Perhaps *The Scarlet Letter* is so popular, generation after
generation, because its beauty lies in the layers of meaning and the
uncertainties and ambiguities of the symbols and characters. Each generation can interpret it and see relevance in its subtle meanings and
appreciate the genius lying behind what many critics call "the perfect
book."

An interest in the past was not new to Hawthorne. As a boy, he had read novelists, such as James Fenimore Cooper and Sir Walter Scott, who wrote historical romances. Although the past appeared an appropriate subject for romance, Hawthorne wanted to go beyond the shallow characters of his predecessors' books and create what he called a "psychological romance"—one that would contain all the conventional techniques of romance but add deep, probing portraits of human beings in conflict with themselves.

Complementing this intriguing theory of a new type of romance, Hawthorne's writing prior to 1850 hinted at the masterpiece yet to come. In "The Gentle Boy," he wrote of an emotional creature faced with the hostility of Puritans, who did not understand emotions. The ambiguity of sin was the subject of still another story, "Young Goodman Brown." These stories helped Hawthorne develop some of the themes that would become part of *The Scarlet Letter*. Two other stories that would predate the conflict of head and heart in his novel were "Rappaccini's Daughter" and "The Birthmark." The cold intellect of Chillingworth, man of science, can be seen in the earlier conflict of these two stories. Both concern men of science or cold intellect who lack human sympathy and compassion and so sacrifice loved ones. This idea was further developed in "Ethan Brand," a study in the conflict of head and heart. In this story, Hawthorne defined the unpardonable sin as the domination of intellect over emotion. He was to develop this idea in *The Scarlet Letter* with his portrayal of Chillingworth, the husband who seeks revenge.

In *The Scarlet Letter*, the reader should be prepared to meet the real and the unreal, the actual and the imaginary, the probable and the improbable, all seen in the moonlight with the warmer light of a coal fire changing their hues. What is Truth and what is Imagination? This is the Boston of the Puritans: Bible-reading, rule making, judgment framing. Surrounding it is the forest of the Devil, dark, shadowy, momentarily filled with sunlight, but always the home of those who would break the rules and those who listen to their passions. Enter this setting with Hawthorne and ample imagination, and the reader will find a story difficult to forget.

A Brief Synopsis

In June 1642, in the Puritan town of Boston, a crowd gathers to witness an official punishment. A young woman, Hester Prynne, has been found guilty of adultery and must wear a scarlet *A* on her dress as a sign of shame. Furthermore, she must stand on the scaffold for three hours, exposed to public humiliation. As Hester approaches the scaffold, many of the women in the crowd are angered by her beauty and quiet dignity. When demanded and cajoled to name the father of her child, Hester refuses.

As Hester looks out over the crowd, she notices a small, misshapen man and recognizes him as her long-lost husband, who has been presumed lost at sea. When the husband sees Hester's shame, he asks a man in the crowd about her and is told the story of his wife's adultery. He angrily exclaims that the child's father, the partner in the adulterous act, should also be punished and vows to find the man. He chooses a new name—Roger Chillingworth—to aid him in his plan.

Reverend John Wilson and the minister of her church, Arthur Dimmesdale, question Hester, but she refuses to name her lover. After she returns to her prison cell, the jailer brings in Roger Chillingworth, a physician, to calm Hester and her child with his roots and herbs. Dismissing the jailer, Chillingworth first treats Pearl, Hester's baby, and then demands to know the name of the child's father. When Hester refuses, he insists that she never reveal that he is her husband. If she ever does so, he warns her, he will destroy the child's father. Hester agrees to Chillingworth's terms even though she suspects she will regret it.

Following her release from prison, Hester settles in a cottage at the edge of town and earns a meager living with her needlework. She lives a quiet, somber life with her daughter, Pearl. She is troubled by her daughter's unusual character. As an infant, Pearl is fascinated by the scarlet *A*. As she grows older, Pearl becomes capricious and unruly. Her conduct starts rumors, and, not surprisingly, the church members suggest Pearl be taken away from Hester.

Hester, hearing the rumors that she may lose Pearl, goes to speak to Governor Bellingham. With him are Reverends Wilson and Dimmesdale. When Wilson questions Pearl about her catechism, she refuses to answer, even though she knows the correct response, thus jeopardizing her guardianship. Hester appeals to Reverend Dimmesdale in desperation, and the minister persuades the governor to let Pearl remain in Hester's care.

Because Reverend Dimmesdale's health has begun to fail, the townspeople are happy to have Chillingworth, a newly arrived physician, take up lodgings with their beloved minister. Being in such close contact with Dimmesdale, Chillingworth begins to suspect that the minister's illness is the result of some unconfessed guilt. He applies psychological pressure to the minister because he suspects Dimmesdale to be Pearl's father. One evening, pulling the sleeping Dimmesdale's vestment aside, Chillingworth sees something startling on the sleeping minister's pale chest: a scarlet *A*.

Tormented by his guilty conscience, Dimmesdale goes to the square where Hester was punished years earlier. Climbing the scaffold, he sees Hester and Pearl and calls to them to join him. He admits his guilt to them but cannot find the courage to do so publicly. Suddenly Dimmesdale sees a meteor forming what appears to be a gigantic *A* in the sky; simultaneously, Pearl points toward the shadowy figure of Roger Chillingworth. Hester, shocked by Dimmesdale's deterioration, decides to obtain a release from her vow of silence to her husband. In her discussion of this with Chillingworth, she tells him his obsession with revenge must be stopped in order to save his own soul.

Several days later, Hester meets Dimmesdale in the forest, where she removes the scarlet letter from her dress and identifies her husband and his desire for revenge. In this conversation, she convinces Dimmesdale to leave Boston in secret on a ship to Europe where they can start life anew. Renewed by this plan, the minister seems to gain new energy. Pearl, however, refuses to acknowledge either of them until Hester replaces her symbol of shame on her dress.

Returning to town, Dimmesdale loses heart in their plan: He has become a changed man and knows he is dying. Meanwhile, Hester is informed by the captain of the ship on which she arranged passage that Roger Chillingworth will also be a passenger.

On Election Day, Dimmesdale gives what is declared to be one of his most inspired sermons. But as the procession leaves the church, Dimmesdale stumbles and almost falls. Seeing Hester and Pearl in the crowd watching the parade, he climbs upon the scaffold and confesses his sin, dying in Hester's arms. Later, witnesses swear that they saw a stigmata in the form of a scarlet *A* upon his chest. Chillingworth, losing his revenge, dies shortly thereafter and leaves Pearl a great deal of money, enabling her to go to Europe with her mother and make a wealthy marriage.

Several years later, Hester returns to Boston, resumes wearing the scarlet letter, and becomes a person to whom other women turn for solace. When she dies, she is buried near the grave of Dimmesdale, and they share a simple slate tombstone with the inscription "On a field, sable, the letter A gules."

List of Characters

Hester Prynne A young woman sent to the colonies by her husband, who plans to join her later but is presumed lost at sea. She is a symbol of the acknowledged sinner; one whose transgression has been identified and who makes appropriate, socio-religious atonement.

Reverend Arthur Dimmesdale Dimmesdale is the unmarried pastor of Hester's congregation; he is also the father of Hester's daughter, Pearl. He is a symbol of the secret sinner; one who recognizes his transgression but keeps it hidden and secret, even to his own downfall.

Pearl Pearl is the illegitimate daughter of Hester Prynne and Arthur Dimmesdale. She is the living manifestation of Hester's sin and a symbol of the product of the act of adultery and of an act of passion and love.

Roger Chillingworth The pseudonym assumed by Hester Prynne's aged scholar-husband. He is a symbol of evil, of the "devil's handyman," of one consumed with revenge and devoid of compassion.

Governor Bellingham This actual historical figure, Richard Bellingham, was elected governor in 1641, 1654, and 1665. In *The Scarlet Letter*, he witnesses Hester's punishment and is a symbol of civil authority and, combined with John Wilson, of the Puritan Theocracy.

Mistress Hibbins Another historical figure, Ann Hibbins, sister of Governor Bellingham, was executed for witchcraft in 1656. In the novel, she has insight into the sins of both Hester and Dimmesdale and is a symbol of super or preternatural knowledge and evil powers.

John Wilson The historical figure on whom this character is based was an English-born minister who arrived in Boston in 1630. He is a symbol of religious authority and, combined with Governor Bellingham, of the Puritan Theocracy.

Character Map

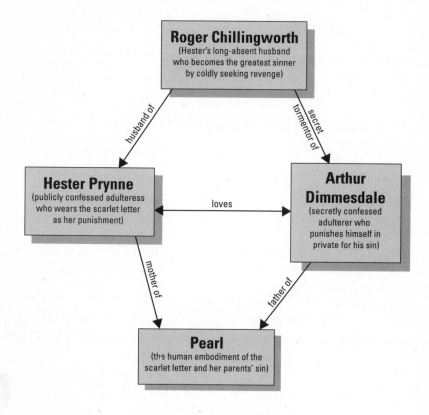

CRITICAL
COMMENTARIES

The Custom House

Summary

Hawthorne begins *The Scarlet Letter* with a long introductory essay that generally functions as a preface but, more specifically, accomplishes four significant goals: outlines autobiographical information about the author, describes the conflict between the artistic impulse and the commercial environment, defines the romance novel (which Hawthorne is credited with refining and mastering), and authenticates the basis of the novel by explaining that he had discovered in the Salem Custom House the faded scarlet *A* and the parchment sheets that contained the historical manuscript on which the novel is based.

Commentary

The preface sets the atmosphere of the story and connects the present with the past. Hawthorne's description of the Salem port of the 1800s is directly related to the past history of the area. The Puritans who first settled in Massachusetts in the 1600s founded a colony that concentrated on God's teachings and their mission to live by His word. But this philosophy was eventually swallowed up by the commercialism and financial interests of the 1700s.

The clashing of the past and present is further explored in the character of the old General. The old General's heroic qualities include a distinguished name, perseverance, integrity, compassion, and moral inner strength. He is "the soul and spirit of New England hardihood." Now put out to pasture, he sometimes presides over the Custom House run by corrupt public servants, who skip work to sleep, allow or overlook smuggling, and are supervised by an inspector with "no power of thought, nor depth of feeling, no troublesome sensibilities," who is honest enough but without a spiritual compass.

A further connection to the past is his discussion of his ancestors. Hawthorne has ambivalent feelings about their role in his life. In his autobiographical sketch, Hawthorne describes his ancestors as "dim and dusky," "grave, bearded, sable-cloaked, and steel crowned," "bitter persecutors" whose "better deeds" will be diminished by their bad ones.

There can be little doubt of Hawthorne's disdain for the stern morality and rigidity of the Puritans, and he imagines his predecessors' disdainful view of him: unsuccessful in their eyes, worthless and disgraceful. "A writer of story books!" But even as he disagrees with his ancestor's viewpoint, he also feels an instinctual connection to them and, more importantly, a "sense of place" in Salem. Their blood remains in his veins, but their intolerance and lack of humanity becomes the subject of his novel.

This ambivalence in his thoughts about his ancestors and his hometown is paralleled by his struggle with the need to exercise his artistic talent and the reality of supporting a family. Hawthorne wrote to his sister Elizabeth in 1820, "No man can be a Poet and a Bookkeeper at the same time." Hawthorne's references to Emerson, Thoreau, Channing, and other romantic authors describe an intellectual life he longs to regain. His job at the Custom House stifles his creativity and imagination. The scarlet letter touches his soul (he actually feels heat radiate from it), and while "the reader may smile," Hawthorne feels a tugging that haunts him like his ancestors.

Literary Device

In this preface, Hawthorne also shares his definition of the romance novel as he attempts to imagine Hester Prynne's story beyond Pue's manuscript account. A careful reading of this section explains the author's use of light (chiaroscuro) and setting as romance techniques in developing his themes. Hawthorne explains that, in a certain light and time and place, objects ". . . seem to lose their actual substance, and become things of intellect." He asserts that, at the right time with the right scene before him, the romance writer can "dream strange things and make them look like truth."

Literary Device

Finally, the preface serves as means of authenticating the novel by explaining that Hawthorne had discovered in the Salem Custom House the faded scarlet *A* and the parchment sheets that contained the historical manuscript on which the novel is based. However, we know of no serious, scholarly work that suggests Hawthorne was ever actually in possession of the letter or the manuscript. This technique, typical of the narrative conventions of his time, serves as a way of giving his story an air of historic truth. Furthermore, Hawthorne, in his story, "Endicott and the Red Cross," published nine years before he took his Custom House position, described the incident of a woman who, like Hester Prynne, was forced to wear a letter *A* on her breast.

Chapter 1
The Prison-Door

Summary

In this first chapter, Hawthorne sets the scene of the novel—Boston of the seventeenth century. It is June, and a throng of drably dressed Puritans stands before a weather-beaten wooden prison. In front of the prison stands an unsightly plot of weeds, and beside it grows a wild rosebush, which seems out of place in this scene dominated by dark colors.

Commentary

In this chapter, Hawthorne sets the mood for the "tale of human frailty and sorrow" that is to follow. His first paragraph introduces the reader to what some might want to consider a (or *the*) major character of the work: the Puritan society. What happens to each of the major characters—Hester, Pearl, Dimmesdale, and Chillingworth—results from the collective ethics, morals, psyche, and unwavering sternness and rigidity of the individual Puritans, whom Hawthorne introduces figuratively in this chapter and literally and individually in the next.

Literary Device

Dominating this chapter are the decay and ugliness of the physical setting, which symbolize the Puritan society and culture and foreshadow the gloom of the novel. The two landmarks mentioned, the prison and the cemetery, point not only to the "practical necessities" of the society, but also to the images of punishment and providence that dominate this culture and permeate the entire story.

The rosebush, its beauty a striking contrast to all that surrounds it—as later the beautifully embroidered scarlet A will be—is held out in part as an invitation to find "some sweet moral blossom" in the ensuing, tragic tale and in part as an image that "the deep heart of nature" (perhaps God) may look more kindly on the errant Hester and her child (the roses among the weeds) than do her Puritan neighbors. Throughout the work, the nature images contrast with the stark darkness of the Puritans and their systems.

Hawthorne makes special note that this colony earlier set aside land for both a cemetery and a prison, a sign that all societies, regardless of their good intentions, eventually succumb to the realities of man's nature (sinful/punishment/prison) and destiny (mortal/death/cemetery). In those societies in which the church and state are the same, when man breaks the law, he also sins. From Adam and Eve on, man's inability to obey the rules of the society has been his downfall.

The Puritan society is symbolized in the first chapter by the plot of weeds growing so profusely in front of the prison. Nevertheless, nature also includes things of beauty, represented by the wild rosebush. The rosebush is a strong image developed by Hawthorne which, to the sophisticated reader, may sum up the whole work. First it is wild; that is, it is of nature, God given, or springing from the "footsteps of the sainted Anne Hutchinson." Second, according to the author, it is beautiful—offering "fragrant and fragile beauty to the prisoner"—in a field of "unsightly vegetation." Third, it is a "token that the deep heart of Nature could pity and be kind to" the prisoner entering the structure or the "condemned criminal as he came forth to his doom." Finally, it is a predominant image throughout the romance. Much the same sort of descriptive analyses that can be written about the rosebush could be ascribed to the scarlet letter itself or to little Pearl or, perhaps, even to the act of love that produced them both.

Finally, the author points toward many of the images that are significant to an understanding of the novel. In this instance, he names the chapter "The Prison Door." The reader needs to pay particular attention to the significance of the prison generally and the prison door specifically. The descriptive language in reference to the prison door—" . . . heavily timbered with oak, and studded with iron spikes" and the "rust on the ponderous iron-work . . . looked more antique than anything else in the New World" and, again, " . . . seemed never to have known a youthful era"—foreshadows and sets the tone for the tale that follows.

Glossary

(Here and in the following chapters, difficult words and phrases, as well as allusions and historical references, are explained.)

Cornhill part of Washington Street. Now part of City Hall Plaza.

Isaac Johnson a settler (1601-1630) who left land to Boston; he died shortly after the Puritans arrived. His land would be north of King's Chapel (1688), which can be visited today.

burdock any of several plants with large basal leaves and purple-flowered heads covered with hooked prickles.

pigweed any of several coarse weeds with dense, bristly clusters of small green flowers. Also called lamb's quarters.

apple-peru a plant that is part of the nightshade family; poisonous.

portal here, the prison door.

Anne Hutchinson a religious dissenter (1591-1643). In the 1630s she was excommunicated by the Puritans and exiled from Boston and moved to Rhode Island.

Chapter 2
The Market-Place

Summary

The Puritan women waiting outside the prison self-righteously and viciously discuss Hester Prynne and her sin. Hester, proud and beautiful, emerges from the prison. She wears an elaborately embroidered scarlet letter *A*—standing for "adultery"—on her breast, and she carries a three-month-old infant in her arms.

Hester is led through the unsympathetic crowd to the scaffold of the pillory. Standing alone on the scaffold as punishment for her adulterous behavior, she remembers her past life in England and on the European continent. Suddenly becoming aware of the stern faces looking up at her, Hester painfully realizes her present position of shame and punishment.

Commentary

Although the reader actually meets only Hester and her infant daughter, Pearl, in this chapter, Hawthorne begins his characterization of all four of the novel's major characters. He describes Hester physically, and he tells about her background, illustrating her pride and shame. Then we see Pearl and hear her cry out when her mother fiercely clutches her at the end of the chapter. Although Pearl is one of the physical symbols of Hester's sin (the other is the scarlet *A*), she is much more than that. She is the product of an act of love—socially forbidden love as it may have been—but love still. This is why Pearl, as we later learn, is not amenable to social rules. She was conceived in an act that was intolerable in the Puritan code and society.

In addition to Hester and Pearl's appearance, we get our first glimpse of the Reverend Arthur Dimmesdale and Roger Chillingworth, the novel's other two main characters. Although the irony of Dimmesdale's relationship to Hester is not yet apparent, his grief over his parishioner Hester is commented on by one of the women assembled near the prison who notes that Dimmesdale "takes it very grievously to heart that such a scandal should have come upon his congregation." And, although Roger Chillingworth is not yet named, we are given a rather full characterization of the man through Hester's recollections of him. He is the "misshapen scholar" who is Hester's legal husband.

Chapter 2 also contains a description of the Puritan society and reveals Hawthorne's critical attitude toward it. The smugly pious attitude of the women assembled in front of the prison who condemn Hester is frightening—especially when we hear them suggest that Hester should be scalded with a hot iron applied to her forehead to mark her as a "hussy," an immoral woman. Although this scene vividly dramatizes what Hawthorne found objectionable about early American Puritanism, he avoids over-generalizing here by including the comments of a good-hearted young wife to show that not all Puritan women were as bitter and pugnaciously pious as these "gossips." The young woman's soft remarks of sympathy for Hester's suffering contrast sharply with the comments of the majority of the women. It is important to note, however, that even this young mother has brought her child to witness the punishment, passing these morals and behaviors to the next generation.

Literary Device

When Hester appears with Pearl, she is in stark contrast to the gloom and the grim reality of the crowd. She has a natural grace and dignity and rejects the arm of the beadle, walking into the sunlight on her own. The most startling part of her appearance is the scarlet letter *A* on her dress. What is meant to be a badge of shame is elaborately decorated in threads of gold. It goes far beyond the standards of richness—sumptuary laws—decreed by the colony. Her extraordinary appearance defies the order of the governor and the ministers. The scarlet letter is "fantastically embroidered and illuminated" and takes "her out of the ordinary relations with humanity" and into a sphere all her own. The red of the letter, standing for adultery, reminds the reader of the rosebush and the letter that later appears in the sky. Its color, for now at least, is associated with her sin and will be strongly connected to Pearl throughout the novel.

Style & Language

Stylistically, the chapter employs a somewhat heavy historical narrative, occasionally interrupted by Hawthorne's comments. It also uses such symbols as the beadle, the scarlet letter *A*, and Pearl. In fact, many of the novel's themes become apparent by investigating the images and symbols represented in the characters, physical objects, and larger social issues. For example, the beadle, or town crier, who carries a sword and walks with a staff symbolic of religious—and therefore social—authority, is described as "grim and grisly." This description also characterizes , both the atmosphere in Chapter 2 and, more important, the society of which the beadle is a part. As the novel progresses, Pearl, the offspring of Hester's adulterous affair, becomes more strongly linked to the scarlet letter *A* that Hester wears on her clothing; likewise, both Pearl's and the A's symbolism are also more fully developed.

Glossary

physiognomies facial features and expression, esp. as supposedly indicative of character.

Antinomian a believer in the Christian doctrine that faith alone, not obedience to the moral law, is necessary for salvation; to the Puritans, the Antinomian doctrine is heretical.

heterodox religious person who disagrees with church beliefs; unorthodox.

petticoat and farthingale underskirts and hoops beneath them.

the man-like Elizabeth Queen Elizabeth I of England (1558-1603), characterized as having masculine qualities.

gossip a person who chatters or repeats idle talk and rumors.

beadle a minor parish officer who keeps order in church.

ignominy shame and dishonor; infamy.

rheumatic flannel material worn to keep warm, especially to ease the pain of rheumatism in the joints.

an hour past meridian 1:00 p.m.

pillory stocks where petty offenders were formerly locked and exposed to public scorn.

Papist a Roman Catholic; the Puritans thought them to be heretics.

spectral of, having the nature of, or like a specter; phantom; ghostly; supernatural.

phantasmagoric dreamlike; fantastic.

Elizabethan ruff an elaborate collar worn around the neck, consisting of tiny accordion pleats.

Chapter 3
The Recognition

Summary

Hester recognizes a small, rather deformed man standing on the outskirts of the crowd and clutches Pearl fiercely to her bosom. Meanwhile, the man, a stranger to Boston, recognizes Hester and is horror-struck.

Inquiring, the man learns of Hester's history, her crime (adultery), and her sentence: to stand on the scaffold for three hours and to wear the symbolic letter *A* for the rest of her life. The stranger also learns that Hester refuses to name the man with whom she had the sexual affair. This knowledge greatly upsets him, and he vows that Hester's unnamed partner "will be known!—he will be known!—he will be known!"

The Reverend Mr. Dimmesdale, visibly upset, pleads with Hester to name her accomplice. He tells her that she should name her partner in sin because perhaps the man doesn't have the courage to step forward even if he wants to. Yet despite Dimmesdale's passionate appeal, followed by harsher demands from the Reverend Mr. Wilson and from a stern voice in the crowd (presumably that of the deformed stranger), Hester steadfastly refuses to name the father of her child. After a long and tedious sermon by the Reverend Mr. Wilson, during which Hester tries ineffectively to quiet Pearl's crying, she is led back to prison.

Commentary

The novel's other two principal characters now make their first physical appearance, and the tensions of the story begin to develop. In Chapter 4, the reader learns that the stranger who so terrifies Hester calls himself Roger Chillingworth, a pseudonym he has chosen for himself. In reality, he is Roger Prynne, the husband whom Hester fears meeting face to face. The other principal character is the young Reverend Dimmesdale, who pleads with Hester to name the father of her infant daughter; Dimmesdale is Pearl's father.

Hawthorne's portrayal of Chillingworth emphasizes his physical deformity. More important, Chillingworth's misshapen body reflects (or symbolizes) the evil in his soul, which builds as the novel progresses. In this chapter, Hawthorne provides hints of just how obsessed Chillingworth will become with punishing Dimmesdale. For example, when Chillingworth recognizes Hester standing alone on the scaffold, "a writhing horror twisted itself across his features, like a snake gliding swiftly over them . . .." Characteristic of Chillingworth, he internalizes "into the depths of his nature" this external convulsion, which will feed his appetite for revenge throughout the novel. The image of the snake is apt when we recall the serpent in the biblical Garden of Eden and the carnal knowledge that it represents. From this chapter forward, revenge and punishment for Dimmesdale will be Chillingworth's only consuming passion.

Dimmesdale's one-paragraph speech to Hester reveals more about his character than any description of his physical body and nervous habits that Hawthorne provides. Knowing that he was Hester's sexual partner and is Pearl's father, the speech that he gives is ripe with double meanings. On one level, he gives a public chastisement of Hester for not naming her lover; on another level, he makes a personal plea to her to name him as her lover and Pearl's father because he is too morally weak to do so himself. Ironically, what is initially intended to be a speech about Hester becomes more a commentary about his own sinful behavior.

In his speech, Dimmesdale asks Hester to recognize his "accountability" in addressing her, and he begs her to do what he cannot do himself. Publicly, he is her spiritual leader, and, as such, he is responsible for her moral behavior. Privately, however, he was her lover, and he shares the blame of the horrible situation that she is in. He then admonishes her, as her spiritual leader, to name her accomplice so that her soul might find peace on earth and, more important, so that she might better her chance for salvation after her death. When he then goes on to "charge" her with naming the transgressor, we understand that he is privately pleading with her to expose him publicly and thereby help ensure *his* salvation, for without public repentance salvation is not attainable.

The dichotomy between Dimmesdale's public speech and personal meaning is most evident in the phrase "believe me." This phrase comes directly following his plea that Hester not take into consideration any feelings she might still have for him. It also follows acknowledgment—

privately to himself, but through public speech—that it would be better for him to step down "from a high place" and publicly stand beside her on the scaffold. Ultimately, his official, public duty and his private, personal intention are one and the same: to admonish Hester to expose her lover's—his own—immorality because he is too morally weak to do so himself.

Glossary

Daniel a prophet from the Old Testament.

Governor Bellingham (1592-1672) the governor of Massachusetts Bay Colony.

halberds combination battle-axes and spears used in the 15th and 16th centuries.

skull-cap a light, closefitting, brimless cap, usually worn indoors.

Chapter 4
The Interview

Summary

Back in her prison cell, Hester is in a state of nervous frenzy, and Pearl writhes in painful convulsions. That evening, when Roger Chillingworth enters Hester's prison cell, she fears his intentions, but he gives Pearl a draught of medicine that eases the child's pain almost immediately, and she falls asleep. After he persuades Hester to drink a sedative to calm her frayed nerves, the two sit and talk intimately and sympathetically, each of them accepting a measure of blame for Hester's adulterous affair.

Chillingworth, the injured husband, seeks no revenge against Hester, but he is determined to discover the father of Pearl. Although this unidentified man doesn't wear a scarlet *A* on his clothes as Hester does, Chillingworth vows that he will "read it on his heart." He then makes Hester promise not to reveal his identity. Hester takes an oath to keep Chillingworth's identity a secret, although she expresses the fear that her vow of silence may prove the ruin of her soul.

Commentary

Unlike the previous chapter, Hawthorne does not summarize or discuss the actions of his characters, nor does he tell the readers what to think. Instead, he puts Hester and Chillingworth together and lets the reader learn about their attitudes and their relationship to each other through their dialogue. By juxtaposing heavily prosaic chapters, like Chapter 3, with ones dominated by the characters' dialogue, Hawthorne creates a pattern in the novel that heightens the dramatic content of the dialogic chapters.

Chapter 4 is especially important to understanding Chillingworth. Hawthorne gives a view of what he has been as well as what he is to become. Throughout the novel, he is referred to as a scholar, a man most interested in studying—reading about—human behavior. Unfortunately, however, Chillingworth hints that in his pursuit of scholarship, he has failed both Hester and himself. He admits to her, "I betrayed thy budding youth into a false and unnatural relation with my decay." We can initially sympathize with this lonely scholar who has been robbed of his wife, but we also can see the element of his future self-destruction in his grim determination to discover the man who has offended him. In fact, as Hester and Chillingworth continue their conversation, we see the development of Chillingworth as one of the novel's symbols of evil.

Of Hester, we learn that she has never pretended to love her husband but that she deeply loves the man whom Chillingworth has vowed to punish. Ironically, it is Hester's concern for Dimmesdale, more than her sense of obligation to her marriage, that persuades her to promise never to reveal that Chillingworth is her husband. This promise will make both Hester and Dimmesdale suffer greatly later in the book.

Glossary

Indian sagamores chiefs or subchiefs in the Abnakis culture.

stripes [Archaic] welts on the skin caused by whipping.

alchemy the ancient system of chemistry and philosophy having the aim of changing base metals into gold.

simples [Archaic] medicines from herbs or plants.

leech [Archaic] a doctor. In Hawthorne's time, blood-sucking leeches were used to effect a cure by removing blood.

Lethe the river of forgetfulness, flowing through Hades, whose water produces loss of memory in those who drink of it.

Nepenthe a drug supposed by the ancient Greeks to cause forgetfulness of sorrow.

Paracelsus (1493-1541) The most famous medieval alchemist; he was Swiss.

bale-fire an outdoor fire; bonfire; here, a beacon fire.

Black Man the devil who "haunts the forest."

Chapter 5
Hester at Her Needle

Summary

Her term of imprisonment over, Hester is now free to go anywhere in the world, yet she does not leave Boston; instead, she chooses to move into a small, seaside cottage on the outskirts of town. She supports herself and Pearl through her skill as a seamstress. Her work is in great demand for clothing worn at official ceremonies and among the fashionable women of the town—for every occasion except a wedding.

Despite the popularity of her sewing, however, Hester is a social outcast. The target of vicious abuse by the community, she endures the abuse patiently. Ironically, she begins to believe that the scarlet *A* allows her to sense sinful and immoral feelings in other people.

Commentary

Chapter 5 serves the purposes of filling in background information about Hester and Pearl and beginning the development of Hester and the scarlet as two of the major symbols of the romance. By positioning Hester's cottage between the town and the wilderness, physically isolated from the community, the author confirms and builds the image of her that was portrayed in the first scaffold scene—that of an outcast of society being punished for her sin/crime and as a product of nature. Society views her " . . . as the figure, the body, the reality of sin."

Despite Hester's apparent humility and her refusal to strike back at the community, she resents and inwardly rebels against the viciousness of her Puritan persecutors. She becomes a living symbol of sin to the townspeople, who view her not as an individual but as the embodiment of evil in the world. Twice in this chapter, Hawthorne alludes to the community's using Hester's errant behavior as a testament of immorality. For moralists, she represents woman's frailty and sinful passion, and when she attends church, she is often the subject of the preacher's sermon.

Banished by society to live her life forever as an outcast, Hester's skill in needlework is nevertheless in great demand. Hawthorne derisively condemns Boston's Puritan citizens throughout the novel, but here in Chapter 5 his criticism is especially sharp. The very community members most appalled by Hester's past conduct favor her sewing skills, but they deem their demand for her work almost as charity, as if they are doing *her* the favor in having her sew garments for them. Their small-minded and contemptuous attitudes are best exemplified in their refusal to allow Hester to sew garments for weddings, as if she would contaminate the sacredness of marriage were she to do so.

The irony between the townspeople's condemnation of Hester and her providing garments for them is even greater when we learn that Hester is not overly proud of her work. Although Hester has what Hawthorne terms "a taste for the gorgeously beautiful," she rejects ornamentation as a sin. We must remember that Hester, no matter how much she inwardly rebels against the hypocrisy of Puritan society, still conforms to the moral strictness associated with Puritanism.

Theme

The theme of public and private disclosure that so greatly marked Dimmesdale's speech in Chapter 3 is again present in this chapter, but this time the scarlet *A* on Hester's clothing is associated with the theme. Whereas publicly the letter inflicts scorn on Hester, it also endows her with a new, private sense of others' own sinful thoughts and behavior; she gains a "sympathetic knowledge of the hidden sin in other hearts." The scarlet letter—what it represents—separates Hester from society, but it enables her to recognize sin in the very same society that banishes her. Hawthorne uses this dichotomy to point out the hypocritical nature of Puritanism: Those who condemn Hester are themselves condemnable according to their own set of values. Similar to Hester's becoming a living symbol of immoral behavior, the scarlet *A* becomes an object with a life seemingly its own: Whenever Hester is in the presence of a person who is masking a personal sin, "the red infamy upon her breast would give a sympathetic throb."

Literary Device

In the Custom House preface, Hawthorne describes his penchant for mixing fantasy with fact, and this technique is evident in his treatment of the scarlet *A*. In physical terms, this emblem is only so much fabric and thread. But Hawthorne's use of the symbol at various points in the story adds a dimension of fantasy to factual description. In the Custom House, Hawthorne claims to have "experienced a sensation . . . as if the letter were not of red cloth, but red-hot iron." Similarly, here in Chapter 5, he suggests that, at least according to some townspeople, the scarlet *A* literally sears Hester's chest and that, "red-hot with infernal fire," it glows in the dark at night. These accounts create doubt in the reader's mind regarding the true nature and function of the symbol. Hawthornes' imbuing the scarlet *A* with characteristics that are both fantastical and symbolic is evident throughout the novel—particularly when Chillingworth sees a scarlet *A* emblazoned on Dimmesdale's bare chest and when townspeople see a giant scarlet *A* in the sky—and is a technique common to the romance genre.

Glossary

ordinations regulations, laws.

sumptuary laws laws set up by the colony concerning expenses for personal items like clothing.

plebeian order the commoners.

emolument profit that comes from employment or political office.

a rich, voluptuous, Oriental characteristic the gorgeous, exquisite, exotically beautiful.

contumaciously disobedient stubbornly resisting authority.

talisman anything thought to have magic power; a charm.

Chapter 6
Pearl

Summary

During her first three years, Pearl, who is so named because she came "of great price," grows into a physically beautiful, vigorous, and graceful little girl. She is radiant in the rich and elaborate dresses that Hester sews for her. Inwardly, however, Pearl possesses a complex character. She shows an unusual depth of mind, coupled with a fiery passion that Hester is incapable of controlling either with kindness or threats. Pearl shows a love of mischief and a disrespect for authority, which frequently reminds Hester of her own sin of passion.

Because both Hester and Pearl are excluded from society, they are constant companions. When Pearl is on walks with her mother, she occasionally finds herself surrounded by the curious children of the village. Rather than attempt to make friends with them, she pelts them with stones and violent words.

Pearl's only companion in her playtime is her imagination. Significantly, in her games of make-believe, she never creates friends; she creates only enemies—Puritans whom she pretends to destroy. But the object that most captures her imagination is the scarlet letter *A* on her mother's clothing. Hester worries that Pearl is possessed by a fiend, an impression strengthened when Pearl denies having a Heavenly Father and then laughingly demands that Hester tell her where she came from.

Commentary

Character Insight

This chapter develops Pearl both as a character and as a symbol. Pearl is a mischievous and almost unworldly child, whose uncontrollable nature reflects the sinful passion that led to her birth. Pearl's character is closely tied to her birth, which justifies and makes the "other worldliness" about her very important. She is a product and a symbol of the act of adultery, an act of love, an act of passion, a sin, and a crime. Hawthorne, the narrator, states, "[Pearl] was worthy to have been brought forth in Eden; worthy to have been left there, to be the plaything of the angels . . . .." However, she "lacked reference and adaptation to the world into which she was born."

The Puritan community believed extramarital sex to be inherently evil and influenced by the devil, and, because Pearl is a product of her mother's extramarital sex, Hawthorne raises the issue of Pearl's nature. Can something good come from something evil? Is Pearl inherently evil because she was born from what the Puritans conceived to be an immoral, sinful union? Perhaps, thinks Hester, who is fearful at least of such a predetermined outcome. Our modern sensibilities, however, shudder at the implication that an immoral act between two adults necessarily means that a child born from that sexual affair will be inherently evil.

Hawthorne's condemnation of Puritanism continues in this chapter. His strongest rebuttal of the society's self-serving, false piety occurs when he ironically contrasts the Puritan community's treatment of Hester and God's treatment of her. He notes of Hester's fellow citizens, "Man had marked this woman's sin by a scarlet letter, which had such potent and disastrous efficacy that no human sympathy could reach her, save it were sinful like herself." Ironically juxtaposed against the Puritan's sentence that Hester wear the scarlet letter *A* is "God, [who] as a direct consequence of the sin which man thus punished, had given her a lovely child, . . . o be finally a blessed soul in heaven!" The comparison between the community's (Puritan's) and God's responses to Hester's extramarital affair is dramatic.

Glossary

anathemas curses things or persons greatly detested.

sprit elf-like.

gesticulation a gesture, esp. an energetic one.

Luther Martin Luther (1483-1546), the first rebel against Catholicism; leader of the Protestant Reformation in Germany.

Chapter 7
The Governor's Hall

Summary

Hester has heard that certain influential citizens feel Pearl should be taken from her. Alarmed, Hester sets out with Pearl for Governor Bellingham's mansion to deliver gloves that he ordered. More important, however, Hester plans to plead for the right to keep her daughter.

Pearl has been especially dressed for the occasion in an elaborate scarlet dress, embroidered with gold thread. On the way to the governor's mansion, Hester and Pearl are accosted by a group of Puritan children. When they taunt Pearl, she shows a temper as fiery as her appearance, driving the children off with her screams and threats.

Reaching the Governor's large, elaborate, stucco frame dwelling, Hester and Pearl are admitted by a bondsman. Inside a heavy oak hall, Hester and Pearl stand before Governor Bellingham's suit of armor. In its curved, polished breastplate, both Hester's scarlet *A* and Pearl are distorted. Meanwhile, as Hester contemplates her daughter's changed image, a small group of men approaches. Pearl becomes quiet out of curiosity about the men who are coming down the path.

Commentary

Style & Language

In addition to preparing the way for the dramatic and crucial interview to come between Hester and the governor, this chapter displays Hawthorne's imagination in developing Pearl's strange nature and the scarlet symbol. Like a symphony with variations, the assorted scarlet references in this chapter add to the richness of the letter's meaning.

Hester comes to Governor Bellingham's house because she has heard that people—particularly the governor—want to deprive her of Pearl. Once again Hawthorne shows his disdain for the smug attitudes of the Puritans. They reason that their "Christian interest" requires them to remove Pearl—the product of sin—from her mother's influence. If Pearl is "capable of moral and religious growth" and perhaps even salvation, they see it as their "duty" to move her to a more trustworthy Christian influence. Hawthorne chides these self-righteous Puritans and likens their concern to a dispute in Puritan courts involving the right of property in a pig.

Literary Device

Hawthorne also designs this chapter to advance the reader's knowledge of Pearl, both in appearance and actions. She is constant motion with "rich and luxuriant beauty." Her actions are full of fire and passion. When the Puritan children fling mud at Pearl, she scares them off. She is an "angel of judgement," an "infant pestilence." Once her fire is spent, she returns quietly to her mother and smiles. Her actions seem to be preternatural behavior in such a young child. Her scarlet dress, a product of Hester's imagination and needle, seems to intensify her "fire and passion." Pearl's scarlet appearance is closely associated with the scarlet letter on Hester's bosom, and Hawthorne continues this relationship as the novel unfolds.

When Hester is told the governor cannot see her immediately, she firmly tells the servant she will wait. Her determined manner indicates to the servant how strongly she feels about the issue of Pearl's guardianship. Because the servant is new in the community, he has not heard the story of the scarlet letter. The beautifully embroidered emblem on her dress and her determination cause him to think she is a person of some influence. Hawthorne emphasizes the servant's recent arrival to impress upon the reader the well-known nature of the scarlet letter's story.

Bellingham's house is described as a mansion of fantasy: cheery, gleaming, sunny, and having "never known death." It comes to life as the only interior description in the novel. Bellingham's home is a mixture of stern Puritan portraits and Old World comforts. Is it any wonder that the polished mirror of the breastplate on Bellingham's armor plays tricks on the eyes? Here in this fortress of Puritan rules where men will decide her fate, Hester virtually vanishes behind the scarlet *A* in the breastplate's reflection. Even Pearl's naughtiness and impish qualities are exaggerated—at least in Hester's mind—as if to defy the stifling, moralistic atmosphere of this place. The governor and his cronies arrive, and Pearl lets out an eerie scream. Their future approaches.

Glossary

cabalistic figures secret or occult figures.

a folio tome; here, a large book.

Chronicles of England a history of England by Holinshed, written in 1577.

tankard a large drinking cup with a handle and, often, a hinged lid.

steel headpiece, a cuirass, a gorget, and greaves . . . gauntlets here, all parts of a suit of armor.

Pequot war raids on Indian villages by Massachusetts settlers in 1637.

Bacon, Coke, Noye and Finch English lawyers of the 16th and 17th centuries who added to British common law.

exigencies great needs; a situation calling for immediate action or attention.

eldritch eerie, weird.

Chapter 8
The Elf-Child and the Minister

Summary

The group of men approaching Hester and Pearl include Governor Bellingham, the Reverend John Wilson, the Reverend Dimmesdale, and Roger Chillingworth, who, since the story's opening, has been living in Boston as Dimmesdale's friend and personal physician.

The governor, shocked at Pearl's vain and immodest costume, challenges Hester's fitness to raise the child in a Christian way. He asks Reverend Mr. Wilson to test Pearl's knowledge of the catechism. Pearl deliberately pretends ignorance. In answer to the very first question—"Who made thee?"—Pearl replies that she was not made, but that she was "plucked . . . off the bush of wild roses that grew by the prison door."

Horrified, the governor and Mr. Wilson are immediately ready to take Pearl away from Hester, who protests that God gave Pearl to her and that she will not give her up. Pearl is both her happiness and her torture, and she will die before she relinquishes her. She appeals to Dimmesdale to speak for her. Dimmesdale persuades Governor Bellingham and Mr. Wilson that Hester should be allowed to keep Pearl, whom God has given to her as both a blessing and a reminder of her sin, causing Chillingworth to remark, "You speak, my friend, with a strange earnestness." Pearl, momentarily solemn, caresses Dimmesdale's hand and receives from the minister a furtive kiss on the head.

Leaving the mansion, Hester is approached by Mistress Hibbins, Governor Bellingham's sister. Hester refuses the woman's invitation to a midnight meeting of witches in the forest, saying she must take Pearl home, but she adds that, if she had lost Pearl, she would willingly have signed on with the devil.

Commentary

This chapter brings back together the major characters from the first scaffold scene—Hester, Pearl, Dimmesdale, and Chillingworth—as well as representatives of the Church, the State, and the World of Darkness.

Note, too, that underneath the surface action, Hawthorne offers several strong hints concerning the complex relationships of his characters. In Hester's appealing to Dimmesdale for help, in Pearl's solemnly caressing his hand, and in the minister's answering kiss lie solid hints that Dimmesdale is Pearl's father.

Hester calls on her inner strength in her attempt to keep Pearl. She argues quite eloquently that the scarlet letter is a badge of shame to teach her child wisdom and help her profit from Hester's sin. However, Pearl's refusal to answer the catechism question causes the decision of the Church and the State to go against her. Now Hester's only appeal is to Dimmesdale, the man whose reputation she could crush.

Character Insight

Pearl once again reveals her wild and passionate nature. In saying that her mother plucked her from the wild roses that grew by the prison door, she defies both Church and State. While such an answer seems precocious for a small child, the reader must remember that Hawthorne uses characters symbolically to present meaning. Pearl's action recalls Hester's defiance on the scaffold when she refuses to name the father of her child. The dual nature of Pearl's existence as both happiness and torture is restated in Hester's plea, and this point is taken up by Dimmesdale. The minister's weakened condition and his obvious nervousness suggest how terribly he has been suffering with his concealed guilt.

Nevertheless, Dimmesdale adds to Hester's plea when he states that Pearl is a "child of its father's guilt and its mother's shame" but still she has come from the "hand of God." As such, she should be considered a blessing. The minister argues that Pearl will keep Hester from the powers of darkness. And so she is allowed to keep her daughter. Those powers of darkness can be seen in both the strange conversation with Mistress Hibbins and also in the change in Chillingworth.

As if to prove that Hester *will* be kept from the darkness by Pearl, Hawthorne adds the scene with Mistress Hibbins. While Mr. Wilson says of Pearl, "that little baggage has witchcraft in her," Hester says she would willingly have gone with the Black Man except for Pearl.

Character Insight

These dark powers are also suggested by the fourth main character, Chillingworth. The change noted by Hester in Chillingworth's physical appearance, now more ugly and dark and misshapen, is a hint that in the scholar's desire for revenge, evil is winning the battle within him and is reflected in his outward appearance. That Chillingworth is

Dimmesdale's personal physician :and supposed friend gives him the opportunity to apply psychological pressure on the minister. Chillingworth's comment on Dimmesdale's strange earnestness and his statement that he could make a "shrewd guess at the father" suggest that he may already have decided on Dimmesdale's guilt.

The battlefield has been marked: The forces of light and darkness are vying for human souls.

Glossary

King James King James I (1603-1625) of England. He ordered the translation of the Bible, now called the *King James Version*.

John the Baptist the preacher who announced in the Bible the coming of Jesus. He was beheaded by Herod whom he accused of adultery.

John Wilson the Reverend John Wilson (1588-1667), a minster who was considered a great clergyman and teacher. He was a prosecutor of Anne Hutchinson.

physic [Archaic] medicine.

the Lord of Misrule a part acted out in court masques in England during the Christmas season. He was part of a pagan, not Christian, myth.

a pearl of great price see the story in Matthew 13:45-46, about a merchant who sold all his goods for one pearl of great worth, which represents the kingdom of heaven. Wilson is saying here that Pearl may find salvation.

New England Primer a book used to teach Puritan children their alphabet and reinforrce moral and spiritual lessons.

Westminster Catechism printed in 1648, it was used to teach Puritan religious lessons and the pillars of church doctrine.

tithing-men men who collect church taxes.

Chapter 9
The Leech

Summary

Since first appearing in the community, Chillingworth has been well received by the townspeople, not only because they can use his services as a physician, but also because of his special interest in their ailing clergyman, Arthur Dimmesdale. In fact, some of the Puritans even view it as a special act of Providence that a man of Chillingworth's knowledge should have been "dropped," as it were, into their community just when their beloved young minister's health seemed to be failing. And, although Dimmesdale protests that he needs no medicine and is prepared to die if it is the will of God, he agrees to put his health in Chillingworth's hands. The two men begin spending much time together and, finally, at Chillingworth's suggestion, they move into the same house, where, although they have separate apartments, they can move back and forth freely.

Gradually, some of the townspeople, without any real evidence except for the growing appearance of evil in Chillingworth's face, begin to develop suspicions about the doctor. Rumors about his past and suggestions that he practices "the black art" with fire brought from hell gain some acceptance. Many of the townspeople also believe that, rather than being in the care of a Christian physician, Arthur Dimmesdale is in the hands of Satan or one of his agents who has been given God's permission to struggle with the minister's soul for a time. Despite the look of gloom and terror in Dimmesdale's eyes, all of them have faith that Dimmesdale's strength is certain to bring him victory over his tormentor.

Commentary

Theme

The theme of good and evil battling is carried through in Chapter 9, "The Leech," a ponderous and philosophical chapter with little action and much positioning of characters. We see the double meaning of the word "leech," the decline of Dimmesdale under his weight of guilt, the development of his relationship with Chillingworth, and the point of view of the townspeople, which have strikingly opposing opinions about the influence of Chillingworth on the minister. As he ingratiates himself with the young minister, and the town sees Chillingworth as "a brilliant acquisition." On the other hand, they suspect that the relationship and proximity of Chillingworth and Dimmesdale have led to Dimmesdale's deterioration.

Hawthorne purposely uses the old-fashioned term "leech" for "physician" because of its obvious double meaning. As a doctor, Chillingworth seems to be making complicated medicines that he learned at the feet of the Indians; he also appears to be sucking the life out of Dimmesdale.

Chillingworth's devious and evil nature is developed in this chapter. As he moves into a home with Dimmesdale and the two freely discuss their concerns, there begins to develop "a kind of intimacy" between them. To Dimmesdale, Chillingworth is the "sympathetic" listener and intellectual whose mind and interests appeal to him. The reader, however, is told that, from the time Chillingworth arrived in Boston, he has "a new purpose, dark, it is true." As Chillingworth becomes more and more absorbed in practicing "the black art," the townspeople notice the physical changes in him, and they begin to see "something ugly and evil in his face." His laboratory seems to be warmed with "infernal fuel," and the fire, which also leaves a sooty film on the physician's face, appears to come from hell.

As the people in town watch this struggle, they feel that this disciple of Satan cannot win and that the goodness of Dimmesdale will prevail. Dimmesdale, however, is not so sure. Each Sunday, he is thinner and paler, struggling under the unrevealed guilt of his deed. The occasional habit of pressing his hand to his ailing heart has now become a constant gesture. He turns down suggestions of a wife as a helpmate, and some parishioners associate his illness with his strong devotion to God. Dimmesdale, although he discusses the secrets of his soul with his physician, never reveals the ultimate secret that Chillingworth is obsessed with hearing. Their relationship is further explored in the next few chapters.

Glossary

appellation a name or title that describes or identifies a person or thing.

ignominious shameful; dishonorable; disgraceful.

deportment the manner of conducting or bearing oneself; behavior; demeanor.

Elixir of Life a subject of myth, a substance that was supposed to extend life indefinitely.

pharmacopoeia a stock of drugs.

Oxford Oxford University in England.

importunate urgent or persistent in asking or demanding; insistent; refusing to be denied; annoyingly urgent or persistent.

New Jerusalem might mean Boston, the city on the hill.

healing balm an ointment used for healing.

Gobelin looms a tapestry factory in Paris that made the finest tapestries.

David and Bathsheba the biblical story of King David's adultery with Bathsheba.

Nathan the Prophet the biblical prophet who condemned David's adultery.

erudition learning acquired by reading and study; scholarship.

vilified defamed or abused.

commodiousness the condition of having plenty of room; spaciousness.

Sir Thomas Overbury and Dr. Forman the subjects of an adultery scandal in 1615 in England. Dr. Forman was charged with trying to poison his adulterous wife and her lover. Overbury was a friend of the lover and was perhaps poisoned.

Chapter 10
The Leech and His Patient

Summary

In this and the next few chapters, Chillingworth investigates the identity of Pearl's father for the sole purpose of taking revenge. Adopting the attitude of a judge seeking truth and justice, he quickly becomes fiercely obsessed by his search into Dimmesdale's heart. He is frequently discouraged in his attempts to pry loose Dimmesdale's secret, but he always returns to his "digging" with all his intelligence and passion.

Most of Chapter 10 concerns the pulling and tugging by Chillingworth at the heart and soul of Dimmesdale. One day in Chillingworth's study, they are interrupted in their earnest discussion by Pearl and Hester's voices outside in the graveyard. They comment on Pearl's strange behavior and then return to their discussion. Watching Hester and Pearl depart, Dimmesdale agrees with Chillingworth that Hester is better off with her sin publicly displayed than she would be with it concealed.

When Chillingworth renews his probing of Dimmesdale's conscience, suggesting that he can never cure Dimmesdale as long as the minister conceals anything, the minister says that his sickness is a "sickness of the soul" and passionately cries out that he will not reveal his secret to "an earthly physician." Dimmesdale rushes from the room, and Chillingworth smiles at his success.

One day, not long afterward, Chillingworth finds Dimmesdale asleep in a chair. Pulling aside the minister's vestment, he stares at the clergyman's chest. What he sees there causes "a wild look of wonder, joy, and horror," and he does a spontaneous dance of ecstasy.

Commentary

Character Insight

This chapter allows the reader to witness Chillingworth's evil determination to accomplish his revenge on and to increase the painful inner suffering of young Arthur Dimmesdale. The reader is also given the best insight yet into the nature of Dimmesdale's tortured battle with himself. Clearly, the struggle within his soul is destroying him, as evidenced by his physical appearance and his mental anguish, yet he still cannot confess his role in the adulterous affair with Hester. It should be noted that Dimmesdale articulates his justification for his silence, but, in the face of Chillingworth's diabolical logic and questioning intended to manipulate the minister into a confession of his sin, Dimmesdale breaks off the colloquy.

Style & Language

Hawthorne refers in this chapter to Chillingworth's earlier reputation as once a "pure and upright man." His shadowy and fiendish descriptions and images of him, however, further develop his symbolic representation of one who now appears to be doing the work of the devil. Just as he was earlier connected to the devil by soot and fire, now Hawthorne uses an allusion to the door of hell in Bunyan's *Pilgrim's Progress* and a reference to the breach of physician-patient relationship and trust in describing Chillingworth as "a thief entering a chamber where a man lies only half asleep" to further emphasize his evilness.

The methodical and devious scholar argues by example and innuendo that Dimmesdale should not die with sin on his conscience; confession will offer him relief in this life and the next. He further argues that the minister cannot serve his fellow man while he has terrible secrets in his soul. Dimmesdale at first resists these arguments saying that they are all fantasy. He feels that people have been able to help their fellow men despite spotted consciences. The minister is a match for Chillingworth until a new sound enters the room.

Character Insight

Pearl's voice comes through the chamber window. She is skipping about on the gravestones in the cemetery and even dancing on one. While Hester tries to restrain her, Pearl will not be controlled by human rules. She calls out to her mother that the minister is already in the grip of the Black Man, and she mischievously throws the burrs at him that she has been using to decorate her mother's token of sin. Chillingworth says, "There is no law, nor reverence for authority, no regard for human ordinances or opinions, right or wrong, mixed up in that child's composition." Dimmesdale agrees, except that she has "the freedom of a broken law."

Following this interruption, Chillingworth asks if Hester is not better off for having confessed her sin rather than hiding it. The young minister agrees, but remains steadfast in his refusal to confess to an earthly doctor rather than talking with God. Because of Chillingworth's constant probing, Dimmesdale becomes angry and rushes from the room.

Later, the minister is asleep in a chair and Chillingworth makes his dark discovery. The spectacular but mysterious reference to Dimmesdale's chest, at the end of the chapter, is an important "clue" that we should remember when we reach Chapter 23. At this point, Chillingworth has identified his quarry.

In this chapter, Hawthorne further develops an important thematic purpose by establishing a firm connection between the body and the soul, the external representation of the inner character ("A strange sympathy betwixt soul and body"). The reader is explicitly lead to interpret the appearances and actions of the characters symbolically with the description of Chillingworth's appearance and actions as he uncovers the secret that lay on Dimmesdale's bosom. The major characters, in fact, are more important as symbols than real people. If their actions seem extraordinary or preternatural to one's sense of reality, he should look carefully to the development of the symbol where objects "loose their actual substance, and become things of intellect." (See The Custom House commentary.)

Glossary

sexton a church officer or employee in charge of maintenance of the church property.

from Bunyans' awful doorway Bunyan's *The Pilgrim's Progress* was an allegory of the late 1600s; the doorway is the entrance to hell.

dark miner worker of the devil; in this case, Chillingworth.

Holy Writ the Bible.

in Spring Lane a crossroad in downtown Boston.

Chapter 11
The Interior of a Heart

Summary

Feeling that he is in full possession of Dimmesdale's secret, Chillingworth begins his unrelenting torture of the minister, subtly tormenting him with comments designed to trigger fear and agony. Dimmesdale does not realize Chillingworth's motives, but he nonetheless comes to fear and abhor him.

As Dimmesdale's suffering becomes more painful and his body grows weaker, his popularity among the congregation grows stronger. Such mistaken adoration, however, further tortures Dimmesdale and brings him often to the point of making a public confession that he is Pearl's father. The minister's sermons are eloquent, but his vague assertions of his own sinful nature are taken by his parishioners as further evidence of his holiness.

Because Dimmesdale is incapable of confessing that he was Hester's lover and that he is Pearl's father—the one act necessary to his salvation—he substitutes self-punishment. He beats himself with a bloody whip and keeps frequent all-night vigils during which his mind is plagued by frightening visions. On one such night while he is seeking peace, Dimmesdale dresses carefully in his clerical clothes and leaves the house.

Commentary

Character Insight

This chapter and the previous one give an in-depth description of a heart "of human frailty and sorrow." The focus of this chapter continues to be Dimmesdale's painful agony, as he writhes beneath the burden of a guilt he seems powerless to confess. Along with strong characterizations of Dimmesdale and Chillingworth, Hawthorne makes two additions to the plot in this chapter: first, the confirmation that Chillingworth no longer has doubts about the minister's guilt; thus, he has undertaken a planned (and successful) campaign to wreak vengeance on the man who seduced his wife and fathered a child by her; second, a specific statement about the methods and degrees of Dimmesdale's own self-punishment.

Literary Device

Hawthorne's irony is evident again in the clever paradox of Dimmesdale's futile attempts at public confession. His suffering has given him sympathies that cause him to understand the sins of others, which results in eloquent and moving sermons. The more Dimmesdale asserts his own sinfulness, the holier his congregation believes him to be. The clergyman is aware that his inadequate confessions are being misunderstood; in fact, he is consciously taking advantage of that misunderstanding: "The minister well knew—subtle, but remorseful hypocrite that he was!—the light in which his vague confession would be viewed." Thus, his sin is compounded by his actions during his period of psycho-spiritual struggle. Hawthorne ensures that readers' sympathy for Dimmesdale's suffering does not blind them to the fact that the minister is a sinner whose troubles are largely of his own making.

At the same time, the symbol of human evil, Chillingworth, appears more evil than ever in this chapter. Chillingworth, Hawthorne says, is a "poor, forlorn creature . . . more wretched than his victim." His revenge is coming at a cost: He is becoming the personification of evil.

Glossary

Pentecost a Christian festival on the seventh Sunday after Easter; it celebrates the Holy Spirit descending on the Apostles.

a miracle of holiness In a similar story of Hawthorne's, "The Minister's Black Veil," the clergyman experiences a similar sympathy from sharing the sin of his fellow men.

the sanctity of Enoch a man in the Bible who lived to be 365 years old. Enoch was pure enough that he walked with God and went to heaven without having to die first.

Chapter 12
The Minister's Vigil

Summary

After leaving the house, Dimmesdale walks to the scaffold where, seven years earlier, Hester Prynne stood, wearing her sign of shame and holding Pearl. Now, in the damp, cool air of the cloudy May night, Dimmesdale mounts the steps while the town sleeps. Realizing the mockery of his being able to stand there now, safe and unseen, where he should have stood seven years ago before the townspeople, Dimmesdale is overcome by a self-hatred so terrible that it causes him to cry aloud into the night.

Hester and Pearl, who are returning from Governor Winthrop's deathbed, mount the scaffold, and the three of them stand hand-in-hand, Hester and Dimmesdale linked by Pearl. Twice, Pearl asks Dimmesdale if he will stand there with them at noon the next day; the minister says he will stand there with them on "the great judgment day." As he speaks, a strange light in the sky illuminates the scaffold and its surroundings. Looking up, Dimmesdale seems to see in the sky a dull red light in the shape of an immense letter *A*. At the same instant, Dimmesdale is aware that Pearl is pointing toward Roger Chillingworth who stands nearby, grimly smiling up at the three people on the scaffold. Overcome with terror, Dimmesdale asks Hester about the true identity of Chillingworth. Remembering her promise to Chillingworth, Hester remains silent.

After the next morning's sermon, the sexton startles the minister by returning one of his gloves, which was found on the scaffold. ("Satan dropped it there, I take it, intending a scurrilous jest against your reverence.") The sexton also asks about the great red letter *A* that appeared in the sky the past night.

Commentary

This chapter, the second of three crucial scaffold scenes, appears exactly in the middle of the novel. Again, Hawthorne gathers all of his major characters in one place—this time in a chapter so foreboding, so convincing in its psychology, and so rich in its symbolism that it is unquestionably one of the most powerful in the novel.

In his description of Dimmesdale's actions while alone on the scaffold, Hawthorne demonstrates his mastery of psychological realism. The sudden changes in mood that take place in the minister's tired mind, the self-condemnation for his cowardice, the near-insanity of his scream, and his impulse to speak to Mr. Wilson all are developed convincingly. The first scaffold scene took place during the noon hours and concentrated on Hester's guilt and punishment. This second scene, occurring at the midnight hours, puts both "sinners" on the scaffold and concentrates on Dimmesdale's guilt and punishment. All the major characters of the first scene are again present. The town, although present, sleeps or is otherwise unaware of the action.

Previously, we have seen Dimmesdale's conscious mind attempting to reason through the problem of his concealed guilt. In contrast, in this chapter, we see the tortured workings of his subconscious mind, which is the real source of his agony. When Dimmesdale is forced by Pearl's repeated question to bring the issue into the open, his fear of confession still dominates his subconscious desire to confess. Just as the town was asleep earlier and there was "no peril of discovery," now he backs off once again. His two refusals to publicly acknowledge his relationship with Hester and Pearl suggest, perhaps, Peter's first two denials of Christ.

Hawthorne's flair for Gothic detail is demonstrated in the appearance of a spectacular, weird light and the startling revelation of the diabolical Roger Chillingworth, who is standing near the scaffold. However, although both details have the effect of supernatural occurrences, Hawthorne is careful to give a natural explanation for each of them. The light, Hawthorne says, "was doubtless caused by one of those meteors, which the night-watcher may so often observe, burning out to waste."

Of course, the meteor seemed otherwise to those who saw it: "Nothing was more common, in those days, than to interpret all meteoric appearances . . . as so many revelations from a supernatural source." And the question of whether the ominous red *A* appeared at all is ambiguous. Although the sexton refers to the letter, Hawthorne suggests that the *A* may have appeared only in Dimmesdale's imagination:

"We impute it . . . solely to the disease in his own eye and heart, that the minister, looking upward to the zenith, beheld there the appearance of an immense letter." Hawthorne also indicates that the meaning is in the mind of the beholder: The sexton sees it as an *A* for angel because Governor Winthrop had recently become an angel. Similarly, Chillingworth's appearance, although it suggests his knowledge of Dimmesdale's whereabouts, is logically explained by his having attended the dying Governor Winthrop.

Literary Device

As in the first scaffold scene, this chapter abounds in both major and minor symbols: the scaffold itself; Dimmesdale's standing on it; the three potential observers representing Church, State, and the World of Evil; the "electric chain" of Hester, Pearl, and Dimmesdale; Pearl's appeal to Dimmesdale; the revealing light from the heavens; and the variation on the letter *A*.

Glossary

scourge a whip used for flogging.

expiation atonement; to pay a penalty for something.

Geneva cloak a black cloak that Calvinist ministers wore.

cope a vestmentworn by priests for certain ceremonies. Here, anything that covers like a cope, a canopy over, or the sky.

scurrilous vulgar, indecent, abusive.

Governor Winthrop John Winthrop (1588-1649), first governor of Massachusetts Bay Colony.

Chapter 13
Another View of Hester

Summary

Following her conversation with Dimmesdale on the scaffold, Hester is shocked by the changes in him. While he seems to have retained his intelligence, his nerve is gone. He is morally weak, and she can only conclude that "a terrible machinery had been brought to bear, and was still operating on Mr. Dimmesdale's well-being and repose." Hester decides she has an obligation to help this man.

Four years have gone by, and Hester's position in the community has changed: She has been given credit for bearing her shame with courage, and her life has been one of purity since Pearl's birth. While Dimmesdale's sermons have become more humane and praised because of his suffering, Hester's position has risen because of her charity. Her scarlet *A* now stands for "Able." But this has come with a price: no friends, no passion, no love or affection.

Through adversity, Hester has forged a new place for herself on the edge of Puritan society. In contrast, Dimmesdale's mental balance has suffered greatly. Now she must help the man who seems to be on "the verge of lunacy." In fact, she feels it has been an error on her part not to step forward before. So she resolves to speak with her husband.

Commentary

It is important to note the chapter title: "Another View of Hester." This chapter is a discussion of Hester's personality, character, and intellect as well as a summary and an update of her past four years (Pearl is now seven). This "other view" refers to both the changing perception of the Puritan community toward Hester and the narrator's telling description of her.

Hester's position in the eyes of the Puritan community has changed considerably due to her grace and her charity. She has borne her shame and sorrow with great dignity. The town describes her now as one "who is so kind to the poor, helpful to the sick, so comfortable to the afflicted!" Now the scarlet letter has magical qualities, and myths are growing around its power. But this new definition of Hester Prynne is not without a price. Her luxuriant beauty, and the warmth, charm, and passion that she once showed have been replaced by coldness, severity, and drabness. There is no affection, love, or passion in her life. Her humanity has been stripped from her by the severity of her punishment, and her charity and benevolence seem mechanical. No one crosses the threshold of her cottage in friendship. To add to this burden, her daughter seems to have been "born amiss."

Another view of Hester identified in the chapter title is that of the narrator, not the Puritan community. Her life, having "changed from passion and feeling to thought . . . she assumed a freedom of speculation . . . which [the Puritans], had they known it, would have held to be a deadlier crime than that stigmatized by the scarlet letter." The narrator speculates that, had it not been for her responsibilities to little Pearl, Hester "might have come down to us in history, hand in hand with Anne Hutchinson, as the foundress of a religious sect" and quite probably would have been executed for "attempting to undermine the foundations of the Puritan establishment." Tellingly, the narrator remarks, "The scarlet letter had not done its office."

This chapter also describes Hester's motive in speaking with Chillingworth, a conversation that will take place in the next chapter. Having seen the terrible toll Chillingworth is taking on Dimmesdale, she decides that she is partly to blame. Now she must do something to redeem her error in not identifying him to her former lover.

Glossary

pristine original or characteristic of an earlier period.

Chapter 14
Hester and the Physician

Summary

While walking on the peninsula with Pearl, Hester sees Chillingworth and sends Pearl down to play by the seashore while she speaks with her husband. She is surprised at the changes in Chillingworth just as she was shocked by Dimmesdale's spiritual ailment and aging. Realizing Chillingworth is in the grip of the devil, she feels responsible for "another ruin." According to Hester, her promise has caused Chillingworth to do evil to the minister, but Chillingworth denies his role at first. Then he admits that, although he used to be kind, gentle, and affectionate, he now allows evil to use him. The physician believes it his fate to become a fiend. He releases Hester from her promise of silence.

Commentary

Character Insight

During these long seven years, Chillingworth has become obsessed with revenge, and this deadly sin has changed him considerably. He pities Hester because he feels she is not really sinful, and any breach with God's law has been paid many times over by her wearing of the scarlet letter. He further feels that if she had "met earlier with a better love than mine, this evil had not been." On the other hand, he also says it is his fate to change from a "kind, true, just" man to a fiend who does the devil's work.

By placing these two characters together in this chapter without Pearl, Hawthorne shows what the years have done to Chillingworth. We see a side of the old scholar that makes us pity him despite his treatment of Dimmesdale, and we feel that of them all, Hester has paid her dues and deserves our respect.

Chapter 15
Hester and Pearl

Summary

As Chillingworth leaves, Hester recognizes how evil he has become and realizes she hates him. Meanwhile, Pearl has entertained herself quite well: she played with her image in a pool, made boats of birch bark, and threw pebbles at beach-birds. Finally, she uses seaweed to make a scarf and then decorates her bosom with a green letter *A*.

Pearl wants to know what the scarlet letter means. Hester is tempted to tell her because she has no one else in whom she can confide. But despite repeated questions by Pearl, Hester says she wears the letter for "the sake of the gold thread"—the first time she had "been false to the symbol on her bosom." Pearl is not satisfied and continues to question Hester until Hester threatens to shut Pearl in a dark closet.

Commentary

Despite her pity for Chillingworth in Chapter 14, Hester reveals her deep hatred for him in this chapter. She realizes that he set off a chain of events beginning with an unnatural, loveless marriage. "Be it sin or no, I hate the man!" is her final word on the subject. We hear for the first time her thoughts about her marriage to Chillingworth. He spent long hours among his books, emerging to "bask himself in [her] . . . smile." While she used to think of this domestic scene as happy long ago, she now sees how dismal it was and counts it among "her ugliest remembrances."

Theme

By now the careful reader should be examining the differences in the two relationships that are presented in the novel. First, in the Hester-Chillingworth relationship is a marriage accepted and He legal in every way but without love and passion. In the Hester-Dimmesdale relationship is love and passion without marriage. The plot and themes of this novel are set in the Puritan society at the confluence of these two relationships.

Another variation on the scarlet letter occurs in Hester's conversation with Pearl. The pathetic loneliness of Hester's position is obvious as she wonders if she should confide in her daughter. Except for the two men in her life, she has no one to whom she can unburden her mind. Hester is strongly tempted to talk with Pearl but then decides to keep the story to herself.

Glossary

sedulous hardworking and diligent.

deleterious harmful or causing injury.

malignant having an evil influence.

nightshade, dogwood, henbane plants used as poisons and in witches charms.

horn-book a sheet of parchment with the alphabet, table of numbers, etc. on it, mounted on a small board with a handle and protected by a thin, transparent plate of horn. It was formerly used as a child's primer.

precocity matured or developed beyond chronological age.

asperity harshness or sharpness of temper.

Chapter 16
A Forest Walk

Summary

For several days Hester tries unsuccessfully to intercept Dimmesdale on one of his frequent walks along the shore or through the woods. When she hears that he will be returning from a trip, she goes with Pearl into the forest, hoping to meet the minister on his return home. As she and Pearl walk along the narrow path through the dense woods, flickering gleams of sunshine break through the heavy gray clouds above them. Pearl suggests the sunshine is running away from Hester because of the *A* on her bosom. In contrast, Pearl, being a child without any such letter, runs and "catches" a patch of light; then, as Hester approaches, the sunshine disappears.

Pearl asks Hester to tell her about the Black Man. She has heard stories about him and questions Hester about her dealings with him and whether the scarlet letter is his mark. Under Pearl's questioning, Hester confesses, "Once in my life I met the Black Man! . . . This scarlet letter is his mark!"

Having reached the depths of the forest, Hester and Pearl sit on a heap of moss beside a brook. Just then footsteps are heard on the path, and Hester sends Pearl away, but not before the girl asks whether it is the Black Man approaching and whether Dimmesdale holds his hand over his heart to cover the Black Man's sign. Before Hester can answer, Dimmesdale comes upon them. The minister looks haggard and feeble and moves listlessly as though he has no purpose or desire to live. He holds his hand over his heart.

Commentary

This chapter and the four chapters that follow contain the longest section of continuous dramatic action in the book. Although the novel covers seven years, fully one-fifth of its total words are concentrated here, during the action of this single, crucial day. This particular chapter serves primarily to set the stage for the confession to follow. It is also rich in atmosphere and symbolism. The chilly gloom of the forest almost perfectly reflects Hester's state of mind and the mood of the following scene. Nearly every element mentioned in the chapter carries some symbolic significance.

Literary Device

The narrow footpath through the dense forest is suggestive of the "moral wilderness" Hester has been forced to follow for the past seven years. The story of the Black Man and his mark is described as a "common superstition," yet for Hester, the Black Man and his mark have a special, personal meaning. Here Hawthorne connects the letter with the Black Man and eventually with Dimmesdale's burden, and he does so mainly through their conversations.

Character Insight

Hawthorne spends part of this chapter connecting Pearl with nature and the wilderness around them. The brook is suggestive of Pearl, "inasmuch as the current of her life gushed from a well-spring as mysterious, and had flowed through scenes shadowed as heavily with gloom." Pearl, being a product of passion, seems to speak to nature and understand its wildness and beauty. She sees how the sunshine loves her yet disappears for Hester. Added to this insight is the idea that Hester hopes Pearl will never have to wear a scarlet letter, or symbol of a "sinful" act. Pearl has not yet had a grief that will fill her with compassion and sympathy, humanizing her as Hester has been humanized.

In coming conversations between Hester and the minister, the symbols of nature, natural law, and humanity will be placed next to the more artificial laws of Puritan society as Hawthorne develops the conflict between them.

Glossary

Apostle Eliot the Rev. John Eliot who preached to Native Americans near Boston.

scintillating sparkling, bright, witty.

scrofula a tuberculosis of the lymph glands in the neck.

Chapter 17
The Pastor and His Parishioner

Summary

As Dimmesdale walks in the wilderness, returning from a visit with Apostle Eliot, he hears Hester's voice and is surprised by her presence. At first, he cannot tell whether she is a human or a ghost. In fact, they are both ghosts of their former selves, and their chill hands and hesitant words reveal the strangeness of this meeting.

Both Hester and Dimmesdale talk with each other about the past seven years, and Dimmesdale confesses his misery and unhappiness. While Hester consoles him and mentions people's reverence for him, the minister feels his guilt and hypocrisy even more. He compares his silence with her public confession and realizes how his hidden guilt is tormenting him.

Hester, realizing how deeply her silence has permitted Dimmesdale to be tortured by her husband, seizes the moment to reveal Chillingworth's secret. This torture has led to insanity and "that eternal alienation from the Good and True, of which madness is perhaps the earthly type." Hester also realizes that she still loves Dimmesdale, and she begs his forgiveness for her silence.

The minister reacts to this revelation with anger at first, blaming her for his torture and realizing why he intuitively recoiled from Chillingworth on their first encounter. Hester, who has silently borne the disdain and scorn of the community and who has lived these seven years without human sympathy, cannot bear Dimmesdale's condemnation, and she falls beside him and cries, "Thou shalt forgive me! Let God punish! Thou shalt forgive!" She hugs him with great tenderness and feels such a compassion for his sorrow that her seven years of punishment seem to fall away.

Dimmesdale, for his part, forgives her and asks God to forgive them both. He believes that Chillingworth is the worst sinner of them all because he "violated, in cold blood, the sanctity of the human heart," unlike he and she, who "never did so." They are reluctant to leave this place in the forest because here they find a peace and harmony that they cannot feel in the Puritan community. Dimmesdale fears Chillingworth's course now that he, no doubt, knows "her purpose to reveal his true character," and he asks Hester to give him courage.

Hester's plan is for Dimmesdale to go deeper into the wilderness and live in natural freedom away from the eyes of Puritan society or to return to Europe, where he will be free of "these iron men and their opinions." But Dimmesdale feels he has not the strength to do either. While he falters, Hester encourages him, claiming that he can lead a powerful life for good and still fulfill his mission on earth. When the minister says he cannot do this alone, she tells him she will go with him.

Commentary

This chapter is pivotal in many respects: It advances the plot and characters by revealing Hester and Dimmesdale's feelings of the past seven years and the reawakening of their dormant love. Also in this chapter, Hawthorne reveals his philosophy on punishment and forgiveness: that deliberate, calculated acts of malice are far worse than sins of passion. In this way, Chillingworth is the worst of the three sinners. Finally, the author provides hope that his characters will find an escape, a way out of their earthly torment. He explores the conflict between natural law and Puritan law in their escape plans.

Character Insight

During the past seven years Dimmesdale has been continually tormented by the dichotomy between what he is and what people believe him to be. His parishioners are "hungry for the truth" and listen to his words as if "a tongue of Pentecost were speaking!" But as often as he has confessed his guilt to God, he has not told it to any other human being. He bears his shame alone. Hawthorne contrasts this with Hester's visible sign of her guilt, confession, and hope for redemption. While Hester tries to console the minister and persuade him that he has repented and left his sin behind, Dimmesdale knows that he can go no place without carrying his hidden guilt along.

Theme

Hester realizes that she still loves Dimmesdale, and she courageously tells him this, even as she reveals her silence concerning Chillingworth. Hawthorne contrasts their love—"which had a consecration of its own"—and Chillingworth's revenge and asks the reader which sin is worse. Who has violated God's law with sure and certain knowledge? And whose place is it to provide redemption and forgiveness? While

Hester believes they can outrun "these iron men" with their rules, guilt, and punishment, Dimmesdale is not so sure. Two forms of moral law are at work here—the laws of God and nature and the laws interpreted and written by "these iron men." In the long run, can escaping the rules of man enable them also to do God's will?

Dimmesdale is reluctant to leave because he believes God has given him a post which he must not desert. This wilderness of God's world is in need of his gifts. Hester assures him that he can do God's will in another place—Europe—and it is only the Puritan laws that hold him in bondage. He can "Preach! Write! Act!" and live a true life in Europe instead of dying, as he seems to be doing here in the wilderness, with fear and shame by his side.

Character Insight

Hawthorne shows the relative strengths of his characters in this argument. Hester reaches within herself and uses the strength and inner courage she has relied on over her seven long and lonely years. In fact, for Hester, "the whole seven years of outlaw and ignominy had been little other than a preparation for this very hour." Deep inside, she knows they can leave the Puritan colony and still have a life of spiritual richness. They have paid for their sins and can still respect and uphold God's laws. Dimmesdale, on the other hand, lacks this perspective and Hester's courage, and several times he calls on her for strength.

Glossary

misanthropy distrust or hatred of people.

these iron men here, meaning the stern Puritan forefathers who make the rules.

Chapter 18
A Flood of Sunshine

Summary

The minister takes courage from Hester's strength and resolves to leave the Puritan colony, but not alone. He reasons that if he is doomed irrevocably, why not be allowed the solace of a "condemned culprit before his execution?" Hester agrees with him and casts off the scarlet letter. She takes off her cap and lets down her full, rich, luxuriant hair. Nature reflects on her passionate action by allowing sunshine to burst forth.

Now Hester wants Dimmesdale to know Pearl. He is reluctant at first, but she assures him Pearl will love him. While the child slowly comes toward them, all of nature seems to tag along as her playmate and kindred spirit.

Commentary

This chapter is a variation on the preceding one and develops more fully Hawthorne's contrast between God's laws as interpreted through nature and God's laws as interpreted by man. Dimmesdale is sorely tempted by the idea of fleeing. He is the chief proponent of the religious tenets in this Puritan community (see "The Puritan Setting of *The Scarlet Letter*" in the Critical Essays). Because the Puritans believe that God allows redemption only for the elect and that salvation is attained solely through faith and the gift of divine grace, Dimmesdale rationalizes that he is a doomed soul and is momentarily attracted to "the solace allowed to the condemned culprit before his execution." He feels he is already a condemned.

By removing the symbols of Puritan law (the scarlet letter) and Puritan society (the formal cap that confined her hair), Hester is transformed from the dull, drab, gray "fallen woman" into the passionate, voluptuous human who follows natural law and expresses her love for Dimmesdale. Nature shows its support for her actions as the sunshine follows her. Dimmesdale relies on her to redeem him and believes she can provide the mercy and forgiveness he has not felt at the hands of God. Taking off the scarlet letter, Hester seems to release them both from an earthly prison. But there is one last hurdle to cross: the meeting between Pearl and Dimmesdale.

In this chapter, Hawthorne's descriptions of Pearl reinforce her mysterious and ethereal nature. She is so closely linked with nature that here, in the forest, the sunlight plays with her, and forest creatures (a partridge, a squirrel, a fox, and a wolf) approach her and recognize "a kindred wildness in the human child." Even the flowers respond to her and, as she passes, seem to say, "Adorn thyself with me, thou beautiful child, adorn thyself with me!" Pearl is "gentler here (in the forest) than in the grassy margined streets of the settlement, or in her mother's cottage," reinforcing that she is in accord with the natural world and not the man-made world. If Hester and Dimmesdale are to pass the test of natural law, they must meet with Pearl's approval. That Pearl advances "slowly; for she saw the clergyman" does not bode well for the reunited lovers.

Glossary

effluence   a flowing forth or outward.

anemones and columbines   flowers of the buttercup family.

nymph-child   a young maiden; here, Pearl.

dryad   a nymph living in the forest among the trees.

Chapter 19
The Child at the Brook-Side

Summary

Hester decides the time has come for Dimmesdale to meet Pearl. Hester and Dimmesdale are joined spiritually and genetically to this child, and "in her was visible the tie that united them." While Dimmesdale confesses that he has always been afraid someone would recognize his features in Pearl, Hester simply speaks of Pearl's beauty and sees her as a "living hieroglyphic." Dimmesdale remembers Pearl being kind to him, yet he also feels ill at ease around children and is not very confident about this meeting. Hester, however, assures him that Pearl will love him and that he should be careful not to overwhelm her with emotion.

Pearl moves very slowly toward them, trying to discern her parents' relationship. Dimmesdale senses her hesitation and puts his hand once again over his heart. Seeing the scarlet letter on the ground and her mother's hair sensuously falling about her shoulders, Pearl points her finger, stamps her foot, shrieks, and "bursts into a fit of passion."

Hester's and Dimmesdale's reactions to Pearl's behavior vary. Hester realizes that Pearl recognizes the change in her (the letter is gone from her bosom and her hair is no longer hidden under a cap), and she hurries to fasten the hated badge to her dress and to draw her cap over her hair. She excuses Pearl's actions by saying children cannot abide change easily. Dimmesdale, on the other hand, begs Hester to do whatever will stop this fit and pacify Pearl. As soon as Hester changes her appearance, Pearl willingly comes to her and mockingly kisses the scarlet letter.

Pearl desires the minister to acknowledge her in public. While Hester assures her that this admission will happen in the future, Dimmesdale kisses Pearl's forehead in an attempt to mollify her. Pearl immediately goes to the brook and washes off the kiss. There she remains apart from the adults, and the brook babbles cheerlessly on.

Commentary

Pearl is the one who moves the action in this chapter, and her response to Dimmesdale and Hester together does not foreshadow a happy ending. In fact, more than ever, Pearl is a symbol of the passionate act of her parents. She is a constant reminder of Hester's sin and, if Hester tries momentarily to forget the past, Pearl certainly disapproves. Pearl, throughout the novel, has shown herself to be unamenable to human rules and laws and seems to lack human sympathy.

Character Insight

Pearl, interpreted on one level, acts like a child who has suddenly realized that her world may be changing. On another level, Pearl is one with nature in the wilderness. Her image is reflected perfectly in the brook, which separates her from Hester and the minister, and as she bursts into a fit of passion at the absence of Hester's scarlet letter, " . . . it seemed as if a hidden multitude were lending her their sympathy and encouragement."

Chapter 20
The Minister in a Maze

Summary

Dimmesdale leaves the forest first, almost believing what has transpired has been a dream. When he looks back, he sees Hester weighed down with sadness and Pearl dancing because he is gone. Turning over their plan in his mind, he believes that going to Europe is the better choice. He is not healthy enough to endure a life in the forest converting natives, and Europe offers more civilization and refinement. Furthermore, a vessel currently in the harbor is soon sailing for England, and Hester will discreetly secure their passage for a departure in four days. The timing of the voyage enables him to give the Election Sermon, an opportunity he can use to terminate his career "honorably."

Thus decided, Dimmesdale is a new man. He walks with great energy and sees everything differently. In fact, he sees things so differently that he almost becomes afraid for himself. Three times, he meets people of his congregation, and each time he is tempted to do something terrible. The venerable and upright deacon of his church is narrowly saved from Dimmesdale uttering blasphemy. The eldest dame of the congregation—she who worshiped the minister—is almost treated to a sacrilegious argument against the soul's immortality. And, finally, a sweet, young virgin narrowly escapes a wicked look from her beloved minister. Finally, he barely refrains from teaching bad words to a group of children and trading curses with a sailor.

Mistress Hibbins invites Dimmesdale to the forest and tells him she admires the way he covers up his true feelings during the day. But she knows she will see him in the forest with the Black Man when midnight comes. Dimmesdale hurries home and, because he is agitated, Chillingworth offers to give him some medicine to calm him down. Dimmesdale lies to Chillingworth, telling him that though he knows his medicine is dispensed by a loving hand, he does not need it. Then he goes to his study and furiously writes his Election Sermon.

Commentary

This entire chapter—note the title—focuses on the spiritual battle warring within Dimmesdale. He has been transformed from the weak and dying man who went into the forest. Hawthorne here examines the nature of the fight and interjects his own comments at various points.

When Dimmesdale says that he will leave after his Election Day sermon so that he will be seen as leaving "no public duty unperformed," Hawthorne writes, "No man, for any considerable period, can wear one face to himself, and another to the multitude, without finally getting bewildered as to which may be true." The formerly weak, pitiful Dimmesdale leaves the forest with a new sense of purpose and energy. His thinking has been transformed by his will and that of Hester.

As if possessed, Dimmesdale returns to the town, a man on fire. He is tempted several times by the irrational, wild, blasphemous, and—what Dimmesdale calls "involuntary"—desire to do wicked things to members of his congregation and perfect strangers. Even Mistress Hibbins recognizes him as a kindred spirit. Dimmesdale is the "wretched minister! . . . Tempted by a dream of happiness, he had yielded himself, with deliberate choice, as he had never done before, to what he knew was deadly sin." This choice is taking him down the road to hell and reviving a multitude of sinful impulses from somewhere. Even his affair with Hester seven years before had not been "a deliberate choice" and hence, although a sin, not a deadly one.

Dimmesdale works with great passion on his Election Sermon, putting this new energy to good use. When Chillingworth says that his congregation may find their ill pastor gone the next year, Dimmesdale agrees. In fact he answers Chillingworth, "Yea, to another world" with "pious resignation." Hawthorne's delicious sense of irony is evident when the reader senses that Chillingworth and Dimmesdale are not talking about the same destinations. Why is Dimmesdale so able to lie to his tormenter? Mistress Hibbins would say it is because his soul has been sold. Whatever the reason, it is definitely providing inspiration for the minister's speech.

Glossary

vicissitude unpredictable changes or variations that keep occurring in life, fortune, etc.; shifting circumstances.

vexed distressed, afflicted, or plagued.

disquietude a disturbed or uneasy condition; restlessness; anxiety.

the Spanish Main the Caribbean.

Bristol a British seaport.

Election Sermon the speech given when a governor is installed. It is a great honor to be asked to give this speech.

irrefragable that cannot be refuted; indisputable; impossible to change.

mutability ability to be changed.

obeisance homage, deference.

buckramed having a covering of cloth made stiff with paste.

Ann Turner an alleged witch who supposedly helped in the poisoning in the previously mentioned Overbury case.

the new Jerusalem another name for Boston; also, a place for sinners who have been saved.

the King's own mint-mark here, a mark guaranteeing authenticity.

Chapter 21
The New England Holiday

Summary

Hester and Pearl go to the marketplace to watch the procession and celebration as elected officials assume their offices. Hester thinks about leaving Boston with Dimmesdale and having a life as a woman once again. While she meditates on her future, Pearl, agitated by the crowd and celebration, dances as she waits for the procession. She alone senses Hester's excitement; to other observers, Hester appears to watch the procession passively.

Pearl continues to ask Hester precocious questions. She wants to know about the procession and asks whether the minister will acknowledge them as he did on the midnight scaffold. Hester quiets her and tells her she must not call out to Dimmesdale.

The captain of the Bristol-bound ship sees Hester and tells her that they will have company on their trip to Europe: Roger Chillingworth.

Commentary

Chapter 21 is the first of several chapters that constitute the third scaffold scene and that lead to the climax of the novel. In these chapters, Hawthorne again brings together his main characters and, in these few pages, illustrates the major conflicts in the light of day and in a very public place.

Theme

One of the first issues addressed is the difference in public and private behavior. Hawthorne uses pointed satire when he comments that, on this most festive day, the people "compressed whatever mirth and public joy they deemed allowable to human infirmity; thereby so far dispelling the customary cloud, that, for the space of a single holiday, they appeared scarcely more grave than most other communities at a period of general affliction." Even Hester serves as a solitary example of the difference between the gloom of Puritan outward life and the excitement she feels within. She must show little joy and certainly no indication that she plans to leave the colony with Pearl and Dimmesdale. At the same time, she is exulting in the fact that soon she will no longer have to wear the scarlet letter, that it will be flung to the bottom of the ocean. For a few hours more, however, she must endure her badge of shame until they are safely away.

Literary Device

Pearl's comments are also important in this chapter because they point to the doom facing Dimmesdale unless he publicly repents. She prophetically describes the minister as a "strange, sad man . . . with his hand always over his heart!" She does not understand why the minister cannot acknowledge her or her mother "here, in the sunny day." The reader sees Hawthorne's message: No matter how far away the three may sail or how long they may live, Dimmesdale can never be at peace with Hester or his tortured conscience if he does not confess his part in their sin.

This idea is further demonstrated when Hester discovers that Chillingworth also plans to leave on the ship to Bristol. Perhaps Dimmesdale will be able to outrun his conscience in this life or his Creator's knowledge in the next. It appears, however, that Chillingworth does not plan to allow him escape from punishment wherever he goes on the face of the earth.

Glossary

plebian inhabitants commoners.

draught of the cup of wormwood and aloes symbolically, a cup of bitter herbs; here, representing what Hester feels inside behind her composed face.

Elizabethan epoch the late 1500s, named for Elizabeth I and called the Golden Age in arts and literature.

Cornwall and Devonshire two counties in southwestern England.

aqua-vitae literally, water of life. Here, a strong liquor such as whiskey.

depredations robbing, plundering, laying waste.

probity uprightness in one's dealings; integrity; honesty.

scurvy or ship-fever a disease caused by lack of vitamin C.

mien a way of looking; appearance.

Chapter 22

The Procession

Summary

While Hester ponders Chillingworth's smile, the Election Day procession begins. First music adds a "higher and more heroic air." Then comes a company of gentlemen soldiers, brilliantly garbed. Next are the political dignitaries, stable, dignified, and drawing a reverent reaction from the crowd. Finally comes the minister, Dimmesdale, whose intellectual prowess is mentioned by Hawthorne. He has changed, showing great energy and an air of purpose in his walk and demeanor. His strength is spiritual, and he has an abstracted air as though he hears things not of this earth.

The focus now goes to Hester and her reaction to Dimmesdale. How far away he seems and how remote from the man she met only three days ago in the forest! She realizes what a great gulf there is between them, and she can scarcely forgive him for his remoteness. Even Pearl does not recognize him because he has changed so completely.

Meanwhile, Mistress Hibbins appears and speaks with Hester and Pearl. As Pearl questions Mistress Hibbins about what the minister hides, the witch tells Hester that she knows the minister also has a hidden sin comparable to Hester's scarlet token. When pressed about how she knows this, Mistress Hibbins explains that intuitively recognizing a fellow sinner is not difficult. She leaves, having said that soon the world will know of Dimmesdale's sin.

Now Hester hears the voice of Dimmesdale giving his sermon; while she cannot hear the words, she does hear sympathy, emotion, and compassion mixed with a "low expression of anguish." He may not be telling the world of his sin, but Hester hears the sadness and despair in his tone because she is so in sympathy with his heart.

Then Pearl scampers off through the crowd in her bright red dress and sees the shipmaster, who gives her a message for her mother: Chillingworth has secured passage for himself and Dimmesdale on the ship. When Hester hears this, she glances around the crowd and sees the same faces that were at the first scaffold scene. The chapter ends with the lines

"The sainted minister in the church! The woman of the scarlet letter in the marketplace!" Who would believe "that the same scorching stigma was on them both?"

Commentary

In this chapter, Hawthorne interrupts the plot to comment on the state of politicians in his time. He describes the early politicians of the colony as lacking mental brilliance but full of "ponderous sobriety." They had great fortitude and inner strength, and, in an emergency, they made wise decisions and stood up to any attack on the colony. Hawthorne even feels they would have peers in the Old World who would see in them the same authority as English statesmen. The people revere them in the Puritan colony, but by Hawthorne's time, that esteem had diminished. He writes that the people of the 1600s had a "quality of reverence; which, in their descendants, if it survive at all, exists in smaller proportion, and with a vastly diminished force, in the selection and estimate of public men."

After this pleasant sojourn into seventeenth century politics, Hawthorne turns the focus on Hester. When Hawthorne describes Hester's reaction to Dimmesdale's remoteness, he virtually eliminates the possibility that they have a future together. In her mind, Hester compares Dimmesdale as he appears at the celebration ("He seemed so remote from her own sphere, and utterly beyond her reach") with how he was just three days earlier in the forest ("how deeply had they known each other then!"). She begins to think she must have dreamed that meeting in the forest because now Dimmesdale seems wholly unsympathetic and removed to his Puritan world. While she can still feel his emotions, she also can hardly forgive him for withdrawing from her and their plans to share their lives.

Literary Device

Hawthorne uses Mistress Hibbins to foreshadow the ending and emphasize the intuitive understanding of human hearts. The old witch reveals that the minister's sin will soon be public knowledge and, when pressed by Hester to explain herself, says that the forest leaves its mark on everyone; even without tell-tale signs, such as leaves or twigs in a person's hair, the evidence is in his demeanor. When Pearl asks about sinful secrets, the witch warns the child that she will see the work of the devil "one time or another."

In this passage, Hawthorne not only describes his ideas about sin, temptation, and human frailty, but he also explains the intuitive nature of human knowledge. Dimmesdale may :have removed himself from Hester's emotional sphere on this day, but she has certainly not lost her intuitive connection with him. In his voice, she hears and recognizes the voices of his heart and also the "low expression of anguish." She may not be able to hear his words distinctly, but she can feel his sorrow-laden and guilty heart. In the tone of voice is a plea for forgiveness.

Somehow the two sinners must come together. To move toward the climax, Hawthorne has cut off escape with Chillingworth's actions, and he ends the chapter by describing the saint and the sinner side by side. Although the world remains unaware, the principal characters are moving closer and closer to this revelation.

Glossary

College of Arms a group which approves titles and coats of arms for hereditary aristocracy in England.

Knights Templars a medieval order of knights founded in 1119 in Jerusalem.

morion a hatlike, crested helmet with a curved brim coming to a peak in front and in back, worn in the 16th and 17th centuries.

compeer a person of the same rank or status; equal; peer.

triple ruff an elaborate collar.

neocromancy black magic; sorcery.

plaintiveness melancholy, suffering.

indefatigable untiring; not yielding to fatigue.

disquietude a disturbed or uneasy condition; restlessness; anxiety.

Chapter 23
The Revelation of the Scarlet Letter

Summary

At the end of Dimmesdale's Election Day sermon, the crowd emerges from the church, inspired by powerful words they have just heard from a man whom they feel is soon to die. This moment is the most brilliant and triumphant in Dimmesdale's public life. As the procession of dignitaries marches to a banquet at the town hall, the feelings of the crowd are expressed in a spontaneous shout of tribute to Dimmesdale. "Never, on New England soil, has stood the man so honored by his mortal brethren, as the preacher!" But the shout dies to a murmur as the people see Dimmesdale totter feebly and nervously in the procession. His face has taken on a deathly pallor, and he can scarcely walk. Several people attempt to help him, but the minister repels them until he comes to the scaffold where Hester stands holding Pearl by the hand. There Dimmesdale pauses.

As the minister turns to the scaffold, he calls Hester and Pearl to his side. Suddenly, Chillingworth appears and attempts to stop Dimmesdale, but the minister scorns the old physician and cries out to Hester to help him get up to the scaffold. The crowd watches in astonishment as the minister, leaning on Hester and holding Pearl's hand, ascends the scaffold steps. Chillingworth's face darkens as he realizes that nowhere else but on the scaffold can Dimmesdale escape him.

The minister tells Hester that he is dying and must acknowledge his shame. Then he turns to the crowd and cries out his guilt. He steps in front of Hester and Pearlfate and declares that on his breast he bears the sign of his sin. He tears the ministerial band from his breast and, for a moment, stands flushed with triumph before the horrified crowd. Then he sinks down upon the scaffold.

Hester lifts Dimmesdale's head and cradles it against her bosom. Chillingworth, meanwhile, kneels down and, in a tone of defeat, repeats, over and over, "Thou hast escaped me!" The minister asks God's forgiveness for Chillingworth's sin; then he turns to Pearl and asks for a kiss. Pearl kisses him and weeps.

Dimmesdale, obviously dying now, tells Hester farewell. She asks whether they will spend eternity together. In answer, he recalls their sin and says he fears that eternal happiness is not a state for which they can hope. The minister leaves the matter to God, whose mercy he has seen in the afflictions leading to his public confession. His dying words are "Praised be his name! His will be done! Farewell!"

Commentary

Hawthorne brings all the principal characters together at a third scaffold scene in this chapter, which begins with the triumph of Dimmesdale's sermon and ends with his death.

Dimmesdale's sermon is a personal triumph. In fact, Hawthorne ironically compares him to an angel who had "shaken his bright wings over the people" and "shed down a shower of golden truths upon them." This final irony between his public and private lives is revealed when he confesses his sin on the scaffold to all of the people who think of him as a saint. He gives up everything: his child, his love, his life, and his honor. The relationship to God that he has been preaching about cannot be based on a lie. God sees everything, and Dimmesdale, no matter how hard he has tried, cannot outrun the truth that his conscience and his mind believe. Sailing to Europe will not bring him beyond the reach of God's knowledge.

Not only does Dimmesdale confess, but he must do so alone. Although Hester helps him to the scaffold where she was punished seven years before, she cannot help him make his peace with God. The Church, in the form of Mr. Wilson, and the State, symbolized by Governor Bellingham, both try to hold Dimmesdale up as he approaches the scaffold, but he repels them and goes on alone. He does turn to Hester prior to his death and ask for her strength, guided by God. Having escaped the clutches of Chillingworth, he turns to Hester with "an expression of doubt and anxiety in his eyes." Before actually confessing, he asks her, "Is this not better than what we dreamed of in the forest?" He is asking Hester to confirm the righteousness of this act and explains to her: "For thee and Pearl, be it as God shall order . . . .. Let me now do the will which He hath made plain before my sight." Although Dimmesdale may still doubt his choice and requires Hester's strength, in the end, he leaves his fate to God, trusting that His mercy will be more certain in death than Chillingworth's relentless torment is in life.

Given that he is dying, Dimmesdale asks Hester whether confession is better than fleeing. She has lived for seven long years with the torment of her neighbors and the shame of her scarlet letter. She hurriedly answers him that perhaps the three of them dying together would be preferable, but if Dimmesdale dies alone what will she have? She will have no love, no life other than the loneliness she has already has, and a daughter who will have no father.

Pearl is given the most wonderful gift: a life that is filled with love and happiness. When her father finally publicly acknowledges her, she kisses him and weeps an actual tear. As Hawthorne says, "the spell is broken." There is hope that Pearl will grow up, be able to interact with other human beings, find love, and live a long and happy life.

Chillingworth loses his victory in two ways. First, he no longer has Dimmesdale to torment, and second, he receives Dimmesdale's blessing. Even as he is dying, the minister manages to retain his reverence and his kindness by asking God's forgiveness for Chillingworth. As Hester noted in her husband's changed appearance earlier, revenge is never a positive motive and generally consumes its possessor.

Glossary

the utterance of oracles the telling of wise predictions about the future.

auditors hearers or listeners.

pathos the emotion of compassion.

transitory stay a very brief stay, as in this life compared to an eternal one.

zenith the point directly overhead.

apotheosized elevated to the status of God, glorified, exalted.

fathomless too deep to be measured; incomprehensible.

Chapter 24
Conclusion

Summary

Several versions circulate of what actually transpired in the marketplace. Most people say they saw a scarlet *A* imprinted on Dimmesdale's chest, but there is conjecture as to its origin. Some think the emblem is a hideous torture the minister inflicted on himself, others think it is the result of Chillingworth's drugs, and still others believe it was remorse gnawing its way out of Dimmesdale's conscience. Still other observers claim that the minister's death serves as a parable showing that even the most saintly of us are sinners. Hawthorne puts this latter version down to the loyalty of friends and gives it little credence. He does state that a moral lesson is to be found in the original manuscript from the Custom House. That precept is "Be true! Be true! Be true! Show freely to the world, if not your worst, yet some trait whereby the worst may be inferred!"

In considering which characters follow this caveat, Hawthorne discusses their fates. Chillingworth, consumed by his revenge, shrivels up and vanishes. He leaves Pearl great wealth in his will, and she and her mother disappear, presumably to Europe. After their departure, the legend of the scarlet letter grows. Finally, one day Hester returns alone and inhabits once again the little cottage. She wears gray and reapplies the scarlet *A* to her bosom.

No one knows Pearl's fate, but people assume that she married well and had a family because letters with the seals of heraldry arrive for Hester and articles of comfort and luxury are found in her cottage. Hester is also seen embroidering baby garments; instead of Puritan colors, she uses most un-Puritan-like lavish and rich materials.

Finally, Hester becomes a symbol of comfort and compassion, and upon her death, she is buried in the cemetery near the prison door where she first was incarcerated. While alive, she gives hope and comfort to those who feel sorrow and pain, and, accordingly, the scarlet letter becomes a symbol of help. She becomes a prophet of a better time where human happiness will be easier to obtain than in the rigid rules of Puritan society. When she dies, she is buried next to Dimmesdale. Their graves are slightly apart but with a single gravestone bearing the inscription: "On a field, sable, the letter A, gules."

Commentary

Style & Language

This concluding chapter serves to answer whatever questions the reader may have after the final scaffold scene. As is his fashion, Hawthorne lends his customary ambiguity and vagueness to many of the questions by citing various points of view or options related to incidences without anointing any one of them as true. One such incident involves what people actually saw when Dimmesdale exposed his bosom on the scaffold. He presents several possible versions of the spectators at the scaffold that day including that some saw no letter on Dimmesdale's chest. He attributes this last version to the loyalty of friends to Dimmesdale.

Theme

Hawthorne explains that the moral of the story, gleaned from an old manuscript of testimony of people who had known Hester, is based on "the poor minister's miserable experience, and he states a kind of moral for us: "Be true! Be true! Be true! Show freely to the world, if not your worst, yet some trait by which the worst may be inferred." This often quoted moral about being true to oneself leaves the reader thinking about the characters in the story and which ones were true and what prices they paid.

Chillingworth shrivels up and vanishes because his revenge has consumed him and made him inhuman. Without his victim, he has no reason to live. But Hawthorne also adds mercy to Chillingworth's death: He explains in a lengthy paragraph that love and hate have a lot in common, and perhaps in the next life, both the spurned husband and the minister will rest in peace.

Pearl's fate is most interesting. The reader is never given a confirmed version of her life but is left to believe she lived a long and happy one, married and the mother of children. Hawthorne ironically notes that her rise in wealth certainly elevated her and Hester in the eyes of the colony that once spurned them. And he further adds that she could have married a "Puritan of the most devout nature." Having seen her father, the devout Puritan, one would certainly not wish that fate on Pearl. Hawthorne hints that her life elsewhere is much happier than it would have been had she married in the New World. The tear she shed at Dimmesdale's death was truly evidence that she would grow up to be humane. And her love and generosity toward Hester are obvious.

Finally, Hester's fate ends the book. One might ask why she returns to Boston, the scene of "her sin . . . her sorrow . . . her penitence." Hawthorne leaves the reader, once again, to decide. Perhaps she feels drawn to the place. Why does she resume wearing the scarlet *A?* Is it a sign that she accepts the rigid standards of Puritan society, or is it a sign that she stayed true to herself by daring to live beyond the petty rules of Puritan society? Hawthorne, perhaps, leans toward the latter idea when he views her as a seer of a future age where "a new truth would be revealed, in order to establish the whole relation between man and woman on a surer ground of mutual happiness."

The graceful and dignified woman Hester has become is a survivor through suffering. Now that she has suffered, she can give what Dimmesdale could not: hope to those who are hopeless and help to those who have sorrow and are in trouble. Because her heart has felt these emotions, she is able to comfort others.

Even in death Dimmesdale and Hester are not allowed to mingle their dust. Perhaps Dimmesdale was right in questioning whether they would have a life together beyond this one. While their graves are slightly apart, the last irony is that they share a common tombstone. They could not be together in life, but in death they share a scarlet letter.

Glossary

portent an omen.

nugatory trifling; worthless; invalid.

parable a short, simple story from which a moral or religious lesson may be drawn.

recluse a solitary person; shut away from the world.

stigma mark or brand; usually shameful.

escutcheon a shield or shield-shaped surface on which a coat of arms is displayed.

gules red; a term used in heraldry.

CHARACTER ANALYSES

Hester Prynne

What is most remarkable about Hester Prynne is her strength of character. While Hawthorne does not give a great deal of information about her life before the book opens, he does show her remarkable character, revealed through her public humiliation and subsequent, isolated life in Puritan society. Her inner strength, her defiance of convention, her honesty, and her compassion may have been in her character all along, but the scarlet letter brings them to our attention. She is, in the end, a survivor.

Hester is physically described in the first scaffold scene as a tall young woman with a "figure of perfect elegance on a large scale." Her most impressive feature is her "dark and abundant hair, so glossy that it threw off the sunshine with a gleam." Her complexion is rich, her eyes are dark and deep, and her regular features give her a beautiful face. In fact, so physically stunning is she that "her beauty shone out, and made a halo of the misfortune and ignominy in which she was enveloped."

Contrast this with her appearance after seven years of punishment for her sin. Her beautiful hair is hidden under her cap, her beauty and warmth are gone, buried under the burden of the elaborate scarlet letter on her bosom. When she removes the letter and takes off her cap in Chapter 13, she once again becomes the radiant beauty of seven years earlier. Symbolically, when Hester removes the letter and takes off the cap, she is, in effect, removing the harsh, stark, unbending Puritan social and moral structure.

Hester is only to have a brief respite, however, because Pearl angrily demands she resume wearing the scarlet *A*. With the scarlet letter and her hair back in place, "her beauty, the warmth and richness of her womanhood, departed, like fading sunshine; and a gray shadow seemed to fall across her." While her punishment changes her physical appearance, it has a far more profound effect on her character.

What we know about Hester from the days prior to her punishment is that she came from a "genteel but impoverished English family" of notable lineage. She married the much older Roger Chillingworth, who spent long hours over his books and experiments; yet she convinced herself that she was happy. When they left Amsterdam for the New World, he sent her ahead, but he was reportedly lost at sea, leaving Hester alone among the Puritans of Boston. Officially, she is a widow. While not a Puritan herself, Hester looks to Arthur Dimmesdale for comfort and spiritual guidance. Somewhere during this period of time, their solace becomes passion and results in the birth of Pearl.

The reader first meets the incredibly strong Hester on the scaffold with Pearl in her arms, beginning her punishment. On the scaffold, she displays a sense of irony and contempt. The irony is present in the elaborate needlework of the scarlet letter. There are "fantastic flourishes of gold-thread," and the letter is ornately decorative, significantly beyond the colony's laws that call for somber, unadorned attire. The first description of Hester notes her "natural dignity and force of character" and mentions specifically the haughty smile and strong glance that reveal no self-consciousness of her plight. While she might be feeling agony as if "her heart had been flung into the street for them all to spurn and trample upon," her face reveals no such thought, and her demeanor is described as "haughty." She displays a dignity and grace that reveals a deep trust in herself.

In this first scene, Dimmesdale implores her to name the father of the baby and her penance may be lightened. Hester says "Never!" When asked again, she says "I will not speak!" While this declaration relieves Dimmesdale and he praises her under his breath, it also shows Hester's determination to stand alone despite the opinion of society. Hester's self-reliance and inner strength are further revealed in her defiance of the law and in her iron will during her confrontation with the governor of the colony.

Despite her lonely existence, Hester somehow finds an inner strength to defy both the townspeople and the local government. This defiance becomes stronger and will carry her through later interviews with both Chillingworth and Governor Bellingham. Her determination and lonely stand is repeated again when she confronts Governor Bellingham over the issue of Pearl's guardianship. When the governor determines to take Pearl away from her, Hester says, "God gave me the child! He gave her in requital of all things else, which he had taken from me . . . Ye shall not take her! I will die first!" When pressed further with assurances of Pearl's good care, Hester defiantly pleads with him, "God gave her into my keeping. I will not give her up!" Here Hester turns to Dimmesdale for help, the one time in the novel where she does not stand alone.

Hester's strength is evident in her dealings with both her husband and her lover. Hester defies Chillingworth when he demands to know the name of her lover. In Chapter 4, when he interviews her in the jail, she firmly says, "Ask me not! That thou shalt never know!" In the forest scene, even Dimmesdale acknowledges that she has the strength he lacks. The minister calls on her to give him strength to overcome his indecisiveness twice in the forest and again as he faces his confession on Election Day.

What is the source of this strength? As she walks out on the scaffold at the beginning of the novel, Hester determines that she must "sustain and carry" her burden forward "by the ordinary resources of her nature, or sink with it. She could no longer borrow from the future to help her through the present." Her loneliness is described in the Chapter 5 as she considers how she can support herself and Pearl, a problem that she solves with her needlework. Yet she continues to lack adult companionship throughout her life. She has nothing but her strength of spirit to sustain her. This inner calm is recognized in the changing attitude of the community when they acknowledge that the *A* is for "Able," "so strong was Hester Prynne, with a woman's strength."

A second quality of Hester is that she is, above all, honest: She openly acknowledges her sin. In Chapter 17, she explains to Dimmesdale that she has been honest in all things except in disclosing his part in her pregnancy. "A lie is never good, even though death threaten on the other side!" She also explains to Chillingworth that, even in their sham of a marriage, "thou knowest that I was frank with thee. I felt no love, nor feigned any." She kept her word in carrying her husband's secret identity, and she tells the minister the truth only after she is released from her pledge. This life of public repentance, although bitter and difficult, helps her retain her sanity while Dimmesdale seems to be losing his.

Finally, Hester becomes an angel of mercy who eventually lives out her life as a figure of compassion in the community. Hester becomes known for her charitable deeds. She offers comfort to the poor, the sick, and the downtrodden. When the governor is dying, she is at his side. "She came, not as a guest, but as a rightful inmate, into the household that was darkened by trouble." Yet Hester's presence is taken for granted, and those that she helps do not acknowledge her on the street.

Hawthorne attributes this transformation to her lonely position in the world and her suffering. No friend, no companion, no foot crossed the threshold of her cottage. In her solitude, she had a great deal of time to think. Also, Hester has Pearl to raise, and she must do so amid a great number of difficulties. Her shame in the face of public opinion, her loneliness and suffering, and her quiet acceptance of her position make her respond to the calamities of others.

In the end, Hester's strength, honesty, and compassion carry her through a life she had not imagined. While Dimmesdale dies after his public confession and Chillingworth dies consumed by his own hatred and revenge, Hester lives on, quietly, and becomes something of a legend in the colony of Boston. The scarlet letter made her what she became, and, in the end, she grew stronger and more at peace through her suffering.

Arthur Dimmesdale

Dimmesdale, the personification of "human frailty and sorrow," is young, pale, and physically delicate. He has large, melancholy eyes and a tremulous mouth, suggesting great sensitivity. An ordained Puritan minister, he is well educated, and he has a philosophical turn of mind. There is no doubt that he is devoted to God, passionate in his religion, and effective in the pulpit. He also has the principal conflict in the novel, and his agonized suffering is the direct result of his inability to disclose his sin.

Of the four major characters in this novel, which investigates the nature of evil and sin and is a criticism of Puritan rigidity and intolerance, Dimmesdale is the only Puritan. One really cannot understand Dimmesdale or his dilemma without at least a cursory understanding of the Puritans who inhabited Boston at this time (see the essay "The Puritan Community" in the Critical Essays) and Hawthorne's psychological perspective through which he presents this tragic character.

In Puritan terms, Dimmesdale's predicament is that he is unsure of his soul's status: He is exemplary in performing his duties as a Puritan minister, an indicator that he is one of the elect; however, he knows he has sinned and considers himself a hypocrite, a sign he is not chosen. The vigils he keeps are representative of this inward struggle to ascertain his heavenly status, the status of his very soul. Note that Hawthorne says of Dimmesdale's nightly vigils, which are sometimes in darkness, sometimes in dim light, and sometimes by the most powerful light which he could throw upon it, "He thus typified the constant introspection wherewith he tortured . . .."

Finally, to add to the Dimmesdale dilemma, the Puritans—therefore, Dimmesdale—did not believe that good works or moral living earned salvation for the individual. As Dimmesdale states, "There is no substance in it [good works]." (Hester, who is not Puritan, believes that Dimmesdale's good works should bring him peace.) The Puritan reasoning was that, if one could earn his/her way into heaven, God's sovereignty is diminished. Since God created the soul and infused it in the human body, salvation is predestined. They reasoned that the elect—that is, God's chosen people—would not or could not commit evil acts; they would act the role, as it were; thus, Dimmesdale's dilemma.

As a minister, Dimmesdale has a voice that consoles and an ability to sway audiences. His congregation adores him and his parishioners seek his advice. As a minister, Dimmesdale must be above reproach, and there is no question that he excels at his profession and enjoys a reputation among his congregation and other ministers. His soul aside, he does do good works. His ministry aids people in leading good lives. If he publicly confesses, he loses his ability to be effective in this regard.

For Dimmesdale, however, his effectiveness betrays his desire to confess. The more he suffers, the better his sermons become. The more he whips himself, the more eloquent he is on Sunday and the more his congregation worships his words. Nevertheless, Hawthorne states in Chapter 20, "No man, for any considerable period, can wear one face to himself, and another to the multitude, without finally getting bewildered as to which may be true."

Dimmesdale's struggle is dark and his penance is horrifying as he tries to unravel his mystery. In Chapter 11, "The Interior of a Heart," Dimmesdale struggles with his knowledge of his sin, his inability to disclose it to Puritan society, and his desire for penance. He knows his actions have fallen short of both God's standards and his own, and he fears this represents his lack of salvation. In an attempt to seek salvation, he fasts until he faints and whips himself on the shoulders until he bleeds. But these punishments are done in private rather than in public and do not provide the cleansing Dimmesdale seeks and needs.

As a sinner, he is weakened to temptation. As demonstrated later, his weakened condition makes it easier for him to associate himself with the Black Man in the forest. His congregation expects him to be above other mortals, and his life and thoughts must exist on a higher spiritual plane than others. Accordingly, his wonderful sermons are applauded by all for a reason his listeners don't understand: Sin and agony have enabled the intellectual scholar-minister to recognize and empathize with other sinners.

In the forest scene, Dimmesdale evidently realizes that he is human and should ask forgiveness and do penance openly. On the way home, he sees how far his defenses have been breached by evil. These thoughts explain why he can so easily write his Election Day sermon, which is filled with the passion of his struggle and his humanity.

Dimmesdale's confession in the third scaffold scene and the climax of the story is the action that ensures his salvation. The reader senses that whether chosen or earned, Dimmesdale's salvation is a reality. Having had several opportunities to confess, without success until this scene, true to his nature if not his ministry, he asks God's forgiveness not only for himself, but also for Chillingworth, who confirms the minister's triumph when he laments, "Thou hast escaped me! . . . Thou hast escaped me!" Dimmesdale's confession also brings about Pearl's humane metamorphosis.

In the long run, Dimmesdale has not the strength of Hester Prynne or her honesty. He cannot stand alone to confess. In death, perhaps he will find a gentler judgment that his own or that of his fellow citizens of Boston.

Roger Chillingworth

Roger Chillingworth, unlike Hester and Dimmesdale, is a flat character. While he develops from a kind scholar into an obsessed fiend, he is less of a character and more of a symbol doing the devil's bidding. Once he comes to Boston, we see him only in situations that involve his obsession with vengeance, where we learn a great deal about him.

Hawthorne begins building this symbol of evil vengeance with Chillingworth's first appearance (" . . . dropping down, as it were, out of the sky, or starting from the nether earth . . ..") in the novel by associating him with deformity, wildness (the Indians), and mysterious power. Having just ended over a year of captivity by the Indians, his appearance is hideous, partly because of his strange mixture of "civilized and savage costume."

Even when he is better dressed, however, Chillingworth is far from attractive. He is small, thin, and slightly deformed, with one shoulder higher than the other. Although he "could hardly be termed aged," he has a wrinkled face and appears "well stricken in years." He has, however, a look of calm intelligence, and his eyes, though they have a "strange, penetrating power," are dim and bleared, testifying to long hours of study under lamplight.

The reader feels a bit sorry for Roger Chillingworth during the first scaffold scene when he arrives in Massachusetts Bay Colony and finds his wife suffering public shame for an adulterous act. At that point, however, he has several choices; he chooses revenge. His rude awakening is described a second time in Chapter 9 when Hawthorne calls him "a man, elderly, travel-worn, who, just emerging from the perilous wilderness, beheld the woman, in whom he hoped to find embodied the warmth and cheerfulness of home, set up as a type of sin before the people." What should have been a warm and loving homecoming after being apart from his wife has become terrible.

Chillingworth is not a Puritan. While he was a captive of the Indians for "upward of a year," he did not judge them as heathens and infidels, and, unlike the Puritans, he did not seek to convert them. Instead, as the scholar, he studied their knowledge of herbs and medicines to learn. He has, indeed, spent his life as a lonely scholar, cutting himself off when necessary in the quest for knowledge from the world of other men. This study of herbs and medicines later links his work to the "black medicine" and helps him keep his victim alive.

Hawthorne further develops this "other world" involvement—whether fate or predetermined by some higher power—when he describes the physician's appearance as being just in time to "help" Dimmesdale. The Puritans believed that the hand of God, or Providence, was in every event. So Hawthorne skewers their belief in mentioning Chillingworth's arrival when he states, "Individuals of wiser faith, indeed, who knew that Heaven promotes its purposes without aiming at the stage-effect of what is called miraculous interposition, were inclined to see a providential hand in Roger Chillingworth's opportune arrival."

When Chillingworth arrives in the colony and learns of Hester's situation, he leaves her alone nearly seven years as he single-mindedly pursues Dimmesdale. He does, however, see his role in her downfall. Because he married her when she was young and beautiful and then shut himself away with his books, he realizes that their marriage did not follow "the laws of nature." He could not believe she, who was so beautiful, could marry a man "misshapen since my birth hour." He deluded himself that his intellectual gifts dazzled her and she forgot his deformity. He now realizes that from the moment they met, the scarlet letter would be at the end of their path.

His love of learning and intellectual pursuit attracts Dimmesdale. In the New World, men of learning were rare. Hawthorne says, "there was a fascination for the minister in the company of the man of science, in whom he recognized an intellectual cultivation of no moderate depth or scope; together with a range and freedom of ideas that he would have vainly looked for among the members of his own profession." This love of wisdom is what will draw the two men together, thus facilitating Chillingworth's plans.

In Chillingworth, Hawthorne has created the "man of science," a man of pure intellect and reason with no concern for feelings. Notice the "chilliness" of his name. In Chapter 9, Hawthorne describes the scarcity of Chillingworth's scientific peers in the New World: "Skillful men, of the medical and chirurgical profession, were of rare occurrence in the colony." These men of science have lost the spiritual view of human beings because they are so wrapped up in the scientific intricacies of the human body. As a paragon of this group, Chillingworth lives in a world of scholarly pursuits and learning. Even when he was married to Hester, a beautiful, young woman, he shut himself off from her and single-mindedly pursued his scholarly studies.

Once Chillingworth decides to pursue Hester's lover and enact revenge, he pursues this purpose with the techniques and motives of a scientist. Moving in with Dimmesdale he pokes and prods. His hypothesis is that corruption of the body leads to corruption of the soul. "Wherever there is a heart and an intellect, the diseases of the physical frame are tinged with the peculiarities of these [the intellectual thoughts]." In Chapter 9, "The Leech," Chillingworth's motives and techniques are explored. As a scientific investigator, he cold-heartedly and intellectually pursues his lab specimen. Hawthorne says, "Few secrets can escape an investigator, who has opportunity and license to undertake such a quest, and skill to follow it up."

When Chillingworth begins his investigation, he does so as a scientist. Hawthorne writes, "He had begun an investigation, as he imagined, with the severe and equal integrity of a judge, desirous only of truth, even as if the question involved no more than the air-drawn lines and figures of a geometrical problem, instead of human passions, and wrongs inflicted on itself." Here the cold intellect of the publicly emerging nineteenth century scientist is used as a framework for Chillingworth's pursuit. This is what makes Chillingworth diabolical and, in Hawthorne's eyes, the greatest sinner. He violates Dimmesdale's heart and soul to see how he will react. Of human compassion, he has none. Eventually when Hester talks with him about whether Dimmesdale's debt has been paid, Chillingworth says that it would have been better had he died than endure seven years of vengeance.

Hawthorne also uses Hester to show what has happened to Chillingworth in isolating himself from humanity. In Chapter 14, she agrees with his description of what he used to be and counters with what he has become. He was once a thoughtful man, wanting little for himself. He was "kind, true, just, and of constant, if not warm affections." But now she tells him that he is a fiend, bent on Dimmesdale's destruction. She says, "You search his thoughts. You burrow and rankle in his heart! Your clutch is on his life, and you cause him to die daily a living death." In Dimmesdale, Chillingworth has a helpless victim, and he exercises his power over the minister with great enthusiasm. He enters Dimmesdale's heart "like a thief enters a chamber where a man lies only half asleep."

By Chapter 14, when Hester meets him in the forest, Chillingworth has a blackness in his visage and a red light showing out of his eyes, as if "the old man's soul were on fire, and kept on smoldering duskily within his breast." In seeking vengeance, he has taken on the devil's job. His obsession with revenge is what makes him—in Hawthorne's eyes—the worst sinner and, therefore, a pawn of the devil. It is appropriate that Hester meets him in the dark forest, a place the Puritans see as the abode of the Black Man. This man of science, so lacking in sentiment, is coldly and single-mindedly seeking what is only God's prerogative: vengeance.

Chillingworth has become such a fiend that his very existence depends on Dimmesdale. When he knowingly smiles to Hester at the Election Day ceremony, he is acknowledging that he, too, will be on that ship bound for Europe, the faithful companion of the minister. It is their fate to be together. When Dimmesdale surprises the physician and climbs the scaffold to confess, Chillingworth knows the minister is about to escape him. His mental torture of the minister is his only reason for living; when his object is beyond reach, Chillingworth does, indeed cease to exist.

In the Conclusion, we discover that Chillingworth "positively withered up, shrivelled away." Obsession, vengeance, and hatred consumed him, but, despite all this, he leaves his fortune to Pearl, a child of love and passion, the living symbol and personification of the scarlet letter. Perhaps this act can, to some degree, redeem the person whose sin was the blackest.

Pearl

Pearl is not meant to be a realistic character. Rather, she is a complicated symbol of an act of love and passion, an act which was also adultery. She appears as an infant in the first scaffold scene, then at the age of three, and finally at the age of seven. (Notice that three and seven are "magic" numbers.)

The fullest description of Pearl comes in Chapter 6. There, we see her at the age of three and learn that she possesses a "rich and luxuriant beauty; a beauty that shone with deep and vivid tints; a bright complexion, eyes possessing intensity both of depth and glow, and hair already of a deep, glossy brown and which, in after years, would be nearly akin to black." We learn further that Pearl has a "perfect shape," "vigor," "natural dexterity," and "a native grace," and that in public she is usually dressed in "gorgeous robes which might have extinguished a paler loveliness."

Her personality is described as intelligent, imaginative, inquisitive, determined, and even obstinate at times. She is a baffling mixture of strong moods, given to uncontrolled laughter at one moment and sullen silence the next, with a fierce temper and a capacity for the "bitterest hatred that can be supposed to rankle in a childish bosom." So unusual is her behavior that she is often referred to in such terms as "elf-child," "imp," and "airy sprite," all of which heighten her symbolism. Governor Bellingham likens her to the "children of the Lord of Misrule," and some of the Puritans believe that she is a "demon offspring."

As a symbol, Pearl functions first as a reminder of Hester's passion. Hester realizes this in the first scaffold scene when she resists the temptation to hold Pearl in front of the scarlet *A*, "wisely judging that one token of her shame would but poorly serve to hide another." As Pearl grows into a lovely, sprite-like child, Hester feels that her daughter's strange behavior is somehow associated with Pearl's conception and birth.

Pearl also functions as a constant reminder of Hester's adulterous act. She is, in fact, the personification of that act. Even as a baby, she instinctively reaches for the scarlet letter. Hawthorne says it is the first object of which she seemed aware, and she focuses on the letter in many scenes. She creates her own letter out of moss, sees the letter in the breastplate at Governor Bellingham's mansion, and points at it in the forest scene with Hester and Dimmesdale.

As a symbol, Pearl always keeps Hester aware of her sin. Just as Dimmesdale cannot escape to Europe because Chillingworth has cut off his exit, Pearl always keeps Hester aware that there is no escape from her passionate nature. The Puritans would call that nature "sinful." In Chapter 6, Hawthorne employs an often-used technique for that passion.

Hawthorne's handling of mirror images has both the goal of representing the passionate, artistic side of man and also the idea that life's truths can be pictured in mirror images. Hester looks into "the black mirror of Pearl's eye" and she sees "a face, fiend-like, full of smiling malice, yet bearing the semblance of features that she had known full well, though seldom with a smile, and never with malice in them." Is this her own face, never with malice, but contorted by the evil of her passion? If so, Pearl is the embodiment of that passion.

The poetic, intuitive, outlawed nature of the artist is an object of evil to the Puritans. As a symbol, Pearl represents that nature. As she looks in the brook in Chapter 19, she sees "another child,—another and the same, with likewise its ray of golden light." This child is an image of Pearl but not quite. Filled with the glory of sunshine, sympathetic, but only "somewhat of its [Pearl's] own shadowy and intangible quality," it is the passion of the artist, the outlaw. This is a passion that does not know the bounds of the Puritan village. In the forest, this passion can come alive and does again when Hester takes off her cap and lets down her hair. Pearl is the living embodiment of this viewpoint, and the mirror image makes that symbol come to life.

Hester herself tries to account for the nature of her child and gets no farther than the symbolic unity of Pearl and her own passion. A close examination of Chapter 6, "Pearl," shows the unification of the child with the idea of sin. Hester is recalling the moment when she had given herself to Dimmesdale in love. The only way she can account for Pearl's nature is in seeing how the child is the symbol of that moment. She recalls " . . . what she herself had been during that momentous period while Pearl was imbibing her soul from the spiritual world, and her bodily frame from its material of earth. The mother's impassioned state had been the medium through which were transmitted to the unborn infant the rays of its moral life; and, however white and clear originally, they had taken the deep stains of crimson and gold, the fiery lustre, the black shadow, and the untempered light of the intervening substance."

Even Pearl's clothes contribute to her symbolic purpose in the novel by making an association between her, the scarlet letter, and Hester's passion. Much to the consternation of her Puritan society, Hester dresses Pearl in outfits of gold or red or both. Even when she goes to Governor Bellingham's to plead for her daughter's custody, Hester dresses Pearl in a crimson velvet tunic. With Pearl's attire, Hester can give "the gorgeous tendencies of her imagination their full play," embroidering her clothes "with fantasies and flourishes of gold-thread." Physical descriptions of Pearl and the scarlet letter are virtually interchangeable.

Mistress Hibbins invites Hester to the forest and Hester says if the governor takes her child away she will gladly go. Their conversation reminds us that, as a symbol, Pearl is also the conscience of a number of people. First, she is the conscience of the community, pointing her finger at Hester. In any number of places, she reminds Hester that she must wear, and continue to wear, the scarlet letter. When they go to the forest and Hester removes the *A*, Pearl makes her put it back on. She tells her mother that "the sunshine does not love you. It runs away and hides itself, because it is afraid of something on your bosom" (Chapter 16).

Pearl is also the conscience of Dimmesdale. In Chapter 3, when Hester stands with her on the scaffold, Pearl reaches out to her father, Dimmesdale, but he does not acknowledge her. Once again on the scaffold in Chapter 13, Pearl asks the minister to stand with them in the light of day and the eyes of the community. When he denies her once again, she washes away his kiss, apt punishment for a man who will not take responsibility. She repeats her request for recognition during the Election Day procession. In her intuitive way, she realizes what he must do so to find salvation.

In the end, it is Dimmesdale's actions that "save" Pearl, making her truly human and giving her human sympathies and feelings. On the scaffold just before his death, Pearl kisses him and "a spell was broken." At that point, Pearl ceases to be a symbol. The great sense of grief, in which the wild infant bore a part, had developed all her sympathies; and as her tears fell upon her father's cheek, they were the pledge that she would "grow up amid human joy and sorrow, nor forever do battle with the world, but be a woman in it."

While Pearl functions mainly as a symbol, she is allowed to become a flesh and blood person at the end. She is a combination of her mother's passion and intuitive understanding and her father's keen mental acuity. In her, Hawthorne has created a symbol of great wealth and layers.

CRITICAL ESSAYS

Symbolism in *The Scarlet Letter*

Nathaniel Hawthorne is one of the most prolific symbolists in American literature, and a study of his symbols is necessary to understanding his novels. Generally speaking, a symbol is something used to stand for something else. In literature, a symbol is most often a concrete object used to represent an idea more abstract and broader in scope and meaning—often a moral, religious, or philosophical concept or value. Symbols can range from the most obvious substitution of one thing for another, to creations as massive, complex, and perplexing as Melville's white whale in *Moby Dick*.

An *allegory* in literature is a story where characters, objects, and events have a hidden meaning and are used to present some universal lesson. Hawthorne has a perfect atmosphere for the symbols in *The Scarlet Letter* because the Puritans saw the world through allegory. For them, simple patterns, like the meteor streaking through the sky, became religious or moral interpretations for human events. Objects, such as the scaffold, were ritualistic symbols for such concepts as sin and penitence.

Whereas the Puritans translated such rituals into moral and repressive exercises, Hawthorne turns their interpretations around in *The Scarlet Letter*. The Puritan community sees Hester as a fallen woman, Dimmesdale as a saint, and would have seen the disguised Chillingworth as a victim—a husband betrayed. Instead, Hawthorne ultimately presents Hester as a woman who represents a sensitive human being with a heart and emotions; Dimmesdale as a minister who is not very saint-like in private but, instead, morally weak and unable to confess his hidden sin; and Chillingworth as a husband who is the worst possible offender of humanity and single-mindedly pursuing an evil goal.

Hawthorne's embodiment of these characters is denied by the Puritan mentality: At the end of the novel, even watching and hearing Dimmesdale's confession, many members of the Puritan community still deny what they saw. Thus, using his characters as symbols, Hawthorne discloses the grim underside of Puritanism that lurks beneath the public piety.

Some of Hawthorne's symbols change their meaning, depending on the context, and some are static. Examples of static symbols are the Reverend Mr. Wilson, who represents the Church, or Governor Bellingham, who represents the State. But many of Hawthorne's symbols change—particularly his characters—depending on their treatment by the community and their reactions to their sins. His characters, the scarlet *A,* light and darkness, color imagery, and the settings of forest and village serve symbolic purposes.

The Characters

Hester is the public sinner who demonstrates the effect of punishment on sensitivity and human nature. She is seen as a fallen woman, a culprit who deserves the ignominy of her immoral choice. She struggles with her recognition of the letter's symbolism just as people struggle with their moral choices. The paradox is that the Puritans stigmatize her with the mark of sin and, in so doing, reduce her to a dull, lifeless woman whose characteristic color is gray and whose vitality and femininity are suppressed.

Over the seven years of her punishment, Hester's inner struggle changes from a victim of Puritan branding to a decisive woman in tune with human nature. When she meets Dimmesdale in the forest in Chapter 18, Hawthorne says, "The tendency of her fate and fortunes had been to set her free. The scarlet letter was her passport into regions where other women dared not tread."

In time, even the Puritan community sees the letter as meaning "Able" or "Angel." Her sensitivity with society's victims turns her symbolic meaning from a person whose life was originally twisted and repressed to a strong and sensitive woman with respect for the humanity of others. In her final years, "the scarlet letter ceased to be a stigma which attracted the world's scorn and bitterness, and became a type of something to be sorrowed over, and looked upon with awe, yet with reverence, too." Since her character is strongly tied to the scarlet letter, Hester represents the public sinner who changes and learns from her own sorrow to understand the humanity of others. Often human beings who suffer great loss and life-changing experiences become survivors with an increased understanding and sympathy for the human losses of others. Hester is such a symbol.

Dimmesdale, on the other hand, is the secret sinner whose public and private faces are opposites. Even as the beadle—an obvious symbol of the righteous Colony of Massachusetts—proclaims that the settlement is a place where "iniquity is dragged out into the sunshine," the colony, along with the Reverend Mr. Wilson, is in awe of Dimmesdale's goodness and sanctity. Inside the good minister, however, is a storm raging between holiness and self-torture. He is unable to reveal his sin.

At worst, Dimmesdale is a symbol of hypocrisy and self-centered intellectualism; he knows what is right but has not the courage to make himself do the public act. When Hester tells him that the ship for Europe leaves in four days, he is delighted with the timing. He will be able to give his Election Sermon and "fulfill his public duties" before escaping. At best, his public piety is a disdainful act when he worries that his congregation will see his features in Pearl's face.

Dimmesdale's inner struggle is intense, and he struggles to do the right thing. He realizes the scaffold is the place to confess and also his shelter from his tormenter, Chillingworth. Yet, the very thing that makes Dimmesdale a symbol of the secret sinner is also what redeems him. Sin and its acknowledgment humanize Dimmesdale. When he leaves the forest and realizes the extent of the devil's grip on his soul, he passionately writes his sermon and makes his decision to confess. As a symbol, he represents the secret sinner who fights the good fight in his soul and eventually wins.

Pearl is the strongest of these allegorical images because she is nearly all symbol, little reality. Dimmesdale sees Pearl as the "freedom of a broken law"; Hester sees her as "the living hieroglyphic" of their sin; and the community sees her as the result of the devil's work. She is the scarlet letter in the flesh, a reminder of Hester's sin. As Hester tells the pious community leaders in Chapter 8, " . . . she is my happiness!— she is my torture . . .. See ye not, she is the scarlet letter, only capable of being loved, and so endowed with a million-fold the power of retribution for my sin?"

Pearl is also the imagination of the artist, an idea so powerful that the Puritans could not even conceive of it, let alone understand it, except in terms of transgression. She is natural law unleashed, the freedom of the unrestrained wilderness, the result of repressed passion. When Hester meets Dimmesdale in the forest, Pearl is reluctant to come across the brook to see them because they represent the Puritan society in which she has no happy role. Here in the forest, she is free and in harmony with nature. Her image in the brook is a common symbol of Hawthorne's. He often uses a mirror to symbolize the imagination of the artist; Pearl is a product of that imagination. When Dimmesdale confesses his sin in the light of the sun, Pearl is free to become a human being. All along, Hester felt there was this redeemable nature in her daughter, and here she sees her faith rewarded. Pearl can now feel human grief and sorrow, as Hester can, and she becomes a sin redeemed.

Chillingworth is consistently a symbol of cold reason and intellect unencumbered by human compassion. While Dimmesdale has intellect but lacks will, Chillingworth has both. He is fiendish, evil, and intent on revenge. In his first appearance in the novel, he is compared to a snake, an obvious allusion to the Garden of Eden. Chillingworth becomes the essence of evil when he sees the scarlet letter on Dimmesdale's breast in Chapter 10, where there is "no need to ask how Satan comports himself when a precious human soul is lost to heaven, and won into his kingdom."

Eventually, his evil is so pervasive that Chillingworth awakens the distrust of the Puritan community and the recognition of Pearl. As time goes by and Dimmesdale becomes more frail under the constant torture of Chillingworth, the community worries that their minister is losing a battle with the devil himself. Even Pearl recognizes that Chillingworth is a creature of the Black Man and warns her mother to stay away from him. Chillingworth loses his reason to live when Dimmesdale eludes him at the scaffold in the final scenes of the novel. "All his strength and energy—all his vital and intellectual force—seemed at once to desert him; insomuch that he positively withered up, shrivelled away, and almost vanished from mortal sight." As a symbol, Chillingworth's job is done.

The Scarlet *A*

Besides the characters, the most obvious symbol is the scarlet letter itself, which has various meanings depending on its context. It is a sign of adultery, penance, and penitence. It brings about Hester's suffering and loneliness and also provides her rejuvenation. In the book, it first appears as an actual material object in The Custom House preface. Then it becomes an elaborately gold-embroidered *A* over Hester's heart and is magnified in the armor breast-plate at Governor Bellingham's mansion. Here Hester is hidden by the gigantic, magnified symbol just as her life and feelings are hidden behind the sign of her sin.

Still later, the letter is an immense red *A* in the sky, a green *A* of eelgrass arranged by Pearl, the *A* on Hester's dress decorated by Pearl with prickly burrs, an *A* on Dimmesdale's chest seen by some spectators at the Election Day procession, and, finally, represented by the epitaph "On a field, sable, the letter A, gules" (gules being the heraldic term for "red") on the tombstone Hester and Dimmesdale share.

In all these examples, the meaning of the symbol depends on the context and sometimes the interpreter. For example, in the second scaffold scene, the community sees the scarlet *A* in the sky as a sign that the dying Governor Winthrop has become an angel; Dimmesdale, however, sees it as a sign of his own secret sin. The community initially sees the letter on Hester's bosom as a mark of just punishment and a symbol to deter others from sin. Hester is a Fallen Woman with a symbol of her guilt. Later, when she becomes a frequent visitor in homes of pain and sorrow, the *A* is seen to represent "Able" or "Angel." It has rejuvenated Hester and changed her meaning in the eyes of the community.

Light and Color

Light and darkness, sunshine and shadows, noon and midnight, are all manifestations of the same images. Likewise, colors—such as red, gray, and black—play a role in the symbolic nature of the background and scenery. But, similar to the characters, the context determines what role the light or colors play. *The Scarlet Letter*'s first chapter ends with an admonition to "relieve the darkening close of a tale of human frailty and sorrow" with "some sweet moral blossom." These opposites are found throughout the novel and often set the tone and define which side of good and evil envelop the characters.

In Chapter 16, Hester and Dimmesdale meet in the forest with a "gray expanse of cloud" and a narrow path hemmed in by the black and dense forest. The feelings of the lovers, weighed down by guilt, are reflected in the darkness of nature. Every so often, sunshine flickers on the setting. But Pearl reminds her mother that the sun will not shine on the sinful Hester; it does shine, however, when Hester passionately lets down her hair. The sun is the symbol of untroubled, guilt-free happiness, or perhaps the approval of God and nature. It also seems to be, at times, the light of truth and grace.

Darkness is always associated with Chillingworth. It is also part of the description of the jail in Chapter 1, the scene of sin and punishment. The Puritans in that scene wear gray hats, and the darkness of the jail is relieved by the sunshine of the outside. When Hester comes into the sunshine from the darkness, she must squint at the light of day, and her iniquity is placed for all to see. Noon is the time of Dimmesdale's confession, and daylight is the symbol of exposure. Nighttime, however, is the symbol of concealment, and Dimmesdale stands on the scaffold at midnight, concealing his confession from the community. In the end, even the grave of Dimmesdale and Hester is in darkness. "So sombre is it, and relieved only by one ever-glowing point of light gloomier than the shadow . . .." The light, of course, is the scarlet letter, shining out of the darkness of the Puritanic gloom.

Colors play a similar role to light and darkness. One of the predominant colors is red, seen in the roses, the letter, Pearl's clothing, the "scarlet woman," Chillingworth's eyes, and the streak of the meteor. At night and always with the physician, the letter is associated with darkness and evil; in the other associations, it is a part of nature, passion, lawlessness, and imagination. The context determines the meaning. Black and gray are colors associated with the Puritans, gloom, death, sin, and the narrow path of righteousness through the forest of sin. Three chapters that contain a multitude of color images are Chapters 5, 11, and 12.

The Setting

Even Hawthorne's settings are symbolic. The Puritan village with its marketplace and scaffold is a place of rigid rules, concern with sin and punishment, and self-examination. Public humiliation and penance are symbolized by the scaffold, the only place where Dimmesdale can go to atone for his guilt and escape his tormentor's clutches. The collective community that watches, at beginning and end, is a symbol of the rigid Puritan point of view with unquestioning obedience to the law. The Church and State are ubiquitous forces to contend with in this colony, as Hester finds out to her dismay. They see Dimmesdale as a figure of public approval, Chillingworth, at least initially, as a man of learning to be revered, and Hester as the outcast. Predominant colors are black and gray, and the gloom of the community is omnipresent.

However, nearby is the forest, home of the Black Man but also a place of freedom. Here the sun shines on Pearl, and she absorbs and keeps it. The forest represents a natural world, governed by natural laws, as opposed to the artificial, Puritan community with its man-made laws. In this world, Hester can take off her cap, let down her hair, and discuss plans with Dimmesdale to be together away from the rigid laws of the Puritans. As part of this forest, the brook provides "a boundary between two worlds." Pearl refuses to cross this boundary into the Puritan world when Hester beckons to her. However, the forest is also a moral wilderness that Hester finds herself in once she is forced to wear the sign of her guilt.

The forest is also a symbolic place where witches gather, souls are signed away to the devil, and Dimmesdale can "yield himself with deliberate choice . . . to what he knew was deadly sin." In these instances, the forest is a symbol of the world of darkness and evil. Mistress Hibbins knows on sight those who would wander "in the forest" or, in other words, secretly do Satan's work. When Dimmesdale leaves the forest with his escape plan in mind, he is tempted to sin on numerous occasions during his journey back to the village. The forest, then, is a symbol of man's temptation.

Every chapter in *The Scarlet Letter* has symbols displayed through characterization, setting, colors, and light. Perhaps the most dramatic chapters using these techniques are the chapters comprising the three scaffold scenes and the meeting in the forest between Hester and Dimmesdale. Hawthorne's ability to introduce these symbols and change them through the context of his story is but one of the reasons *The Scarlet Letter* is considered his masterpiece and a peerless example of the romance novel.

The Puritan Setting of *The Scarlet Letter*

Nathaniel Hawthorne had deep bonds with his Puritan ancestors and created a story that both highlighted their weaknesses and their strengths. His knowledge of their beliefs and his admiration for their strengths were balanced by his concerns for their rigid and oppressive rules. *The Scarlet Letter* shows his attitude toward these Puritans of Boston in his portrayal of characters, his plot, and the themes of his story.

The early Puritans who first came to America in 1620 founded a precarious colony in Plymouth, Massachusetts. While half the colonists died that first year, the other half were saved by the coming spring and the timely intervention of the Indians. These first settlers were followed ten years later by a wave of Puritans that continued in the 1630s and thereafter, until, by the 1640s, New England had over twenty-five thousand English settlers. The second group in the 1630s settled in the area of present-day Boston in a community they named Massachusetts Bay Colony. It is this colony that forms the setting of *The Scarlet Letter*.

The City upon a Hill

The Puritans left the Old World because they wanted to "purify" the Church of England. Their chief complaints were that the services should be simpler and that religion should contain an intense spiritual relationship between the individual and God. In England, the clergy and the government mediated in the relationship between the individual and God. Because the Puritans chose to defy these assumptions, they were persecuted in England. A group of them fled to Holland and subsequently to the New World, where they hoped to build a society, described by John Winthrop, as "a city upon a hill"—a place where the "eyes of all people are upon us." In such a place and as long as they followed His words and did their work to glorify His ways, God would bless them, and they would prosper. Hawthorne, of course, presents the irony of this concept when he describes the prison as a building already worn when the colony is only fifteen years old.

Hawthorne's viewpoint of this society seems to be disclosed in several places in the novel but never more so than in the Governor's house in Chapter 7 and during the New England holiday in Chapter 21. On Bellingham's walls are portraits of his forefathers who wear the stately and formal clothing of the Old World. Hawthorne says that, "All were characterized by the sternness and severity which old portraits so invariably put on; as if they were the ghosts, rather than the pictures, of departed worthies, and were gazing with harsh and intolerant criticism at the pursuits and enjoyments of living men." Obviously, it does not bode well to be too happy in the colony, or reprimand is sure to follow. In the recounting of the New England holiday set aside to honor a change in government, Hawthorne describes the non-Puritan paradegoers in the most joyful of terms. Their dress, their behavior, and even the happiness on their faces is very un-Puritan-like. He writes, with his pointed understatement, that "the Puritans compressed whatever mirth and public joy they deemed allowable to human infirmity; thereby so far dispelling the customary cloud, that, for the space of a single holiday, they appeared scarcely more grave than most other communities at a period of general affliction."

Hawthorne's gift for ironic understatement should be balanced by the sense that he feels connected to his Puritan ancestors and admires a number of their qualities. Consider the description he gives of them in his Custom House preface. He sees them, like the old General he describes, as people of perseverance, integrity, inner strength, and moral courage. He also shares a concern for their disdain toward his need to take on a commercial job that contributes little to the community in spiritual profit. In addition, note Hawthorne's condemnation of the tax supervisor who has no sensibility or spiritual compass.

The Nature of Man and Salvation

These early Puritans followed the writings of a French Protestant reformer named John Calvin (1509-1564), whose teachings saw the world as a grim conflict between God and Satan. Calvinists were a very introspective lot who constantly searched their souls for evidence that they were God's Elect. The Elect were people chosen by God for salvation. According to Puritans, a merciful God had sent His son, Jesus Christ, to earth to die for the sins of man, but only a few would be saved. The rest, known as the "unregenerate," would be damned eternally.

The Puritans who settled Massachusetts Bay Colony believed that all mankind was depraved and sinful because of Adam and Eve's fall in the Garden of Eden. Because Adam and Eve were willful and disobedient to God, they brought upon mankind the curse of depravity, sometimes called Original Sin. For this reason, *The New England Primer* (1683), which was used to teach reading in Puritan schools, began with "A: In Adam's Fall / We sinned all." Most Puritans could be sure of eternal punishment in hell; the few that were "elect" would go to heaven.

The Link between Church and State

Those who were male and members of the church could vote. In addition, ministers guided the elected officials of the colony; consequently, there was a close tie between Church and State. In *The Scarlet Letter,* those two branches of the government are represented by Mr. Roger Wilson (Church) and Governor Bellingham (State). The rules governing the Puritans came from the Bible, a source of spiritual and ethical standards. These rules were definite, and the penalties or punishments were public and severe. Hester's turn on the scaffold and her scarlet letter were similar to those who were branded or forced to wear an *M* for murderer. The stocks were a form of public indictment—and, therefore, deterrent—of bad behavior. Those who disagreed with the laws of the colony were banished, persecuted, and, in some cases, executed.

Obviously, these rigid Puritan standards had both good and bad outcomes. The colony would not have survived without the faith, hard work, courage, and perseverance of these early religious believers. They feared Indian attacks and had to survive lethal diseases, starvation, and the harsh New England winters. They also formed a society in which the rules were very clear. There were few gray areas in the standards of behavior expected by the Puritans and taught early to their children. These stern and introspective Puritans provided a rigid structure that was repressive to the individual but that enabled the colony to survive those early years when order and faith were needed.

On the other hand, the society built by the Puritans was stern and repressive, with little room for individualism. In this society, the "path of righteousness" was very narrow and taught through stern sermons on guilt and sin. The irony, of course, is in the difference between public knowledge and private actions. Dimmesdale and Chillingworth, both "sinners" for their part in this drama, are valued and revered members of this repressive community, while Hester is an outcast because of her publicly acknowledged sin. These "iron men and their rules" provide a backdrop for Hawthorne's story that keeps the conflict alive because public appearances and penance were dramatically important parts of the Puritan community.

In contrast, the forest—seen by the Puritans as the haunt of the Black Man or devil—was a place of little law and order. Those who chose to follow evil signed their name in the Black Man's book and chose a life of sin. Mistress Hibbins symbolizes this world in *The Scarlet Letter*. And, in fact, she says, "Many a church-member saw I, walking behind the music, that has danced in the same measure with me." These Puritans may speak of branding Hester Prynne in one breath but dance to the devil's music in the forest in their next breath. The meeting between Dimmesdale and Hester takes place in the forest, away from the stern, repressive laws of society. There they can discuss a central conflict of the novel: the needs of human nature as opposed to the laws of society. This conflict is seen even in the early chapters.

Punishment

The wrath of the colony toward malefactors is brutally obvious in the first scaffold scene in Chapter 2. The "good women" of the colony discuss the community good that could be realized if they were in charge of public punishment. "At the very least, they should have put the brand of a hot iron on Hester Prynne's forehead." Another woman in the crowd who is the "most pitiless of these self-constituted judges" points to the scriptural basis of their law in the colony: "This woman has brought shame upon us all, and ought to die. Is there not law for it? Truly, there is, both in the Scripture and the statute book. Then let the magistrates, who have made it of no effect, thank themselves if their own wives and daughters go astray!"

The Puritans had great difficulty in loving the sinner and hating the sin in Massachusetts Bay Colony. When Chillingworth asks a person in the crowd about Hester's crime, he is told that the sentence was softened from death by "their [the magistrates and ministers'] great mercy and tenderness of heart" because she is a beautiful widow and probably was "tempted to her fall." The scholar/doctor says this penalty is wise because she will be "a living sermon against sin." The only softening of community opinion is from the young woman in the crowd who says that no matter how Hester might cover the letter on her dress, she will always know inside that she is a sinner.

How do the magistrates and ministers—mighty pillars of the community—feel about Hester's sin and their statutes? In Chapter 3, Hawthorne describes Bellingham and the others sitting around Hester and says that, although they are "doubtless, good men, just and sage," it would be impossible to find men less capable of understanding the behavior of Hester Prynne. Mr. Wilson, representing the religious realm of rule, discusses the "vileness and blackness" of Hester's sin and reports that only the intervention of the minister, Dimmesdale, has persuaded him that the minister is a better judge of arguments that will cause Hester to reveal the name of the child's father. Dimmesdale's voice, which affected his congregation "like the speech of an angel," also exhorts Hester to name the father. In a speech filled with hypocrisy and desiring to force Hester to make the decision about his public confession, he challenges her to reveal his name:

"Be not silent from any mistaken pity and tenderness for him; for, believe me, Hester, though he were to step down from a high place, and stand there beside thee, on thy pedestal of shame, yet better were it so, than to hide a guilty heart through life. What can thy silence do for him, except to tempt him—yea, compel him, as it were—to add hypocrisy to sin? . . . Take heed how thou deniest to him—who, perchance, hath not the courage to grasp it for himself—the bitter, but wholesome, cup that is now presented to thy lips!"

While the community calls for Hester's blood, those who are equally sinful remain silent. The irony of public appearance and private knowledge are themes throughout this story. The only escape from public scrutiny is the forest. The lovers are caught up in a web of lies and deception. They can safely meet and discuss Chillingworth's identity and their plan of escape in the forest, haunt of the Black Man. Here Hester and Dimmesdale plan their escape to Europe where they can follow their hearts and forget the rigid rules of their Puritan society. But the Puritan conscience is too deeply ingrained in Dimmesdale, and though he dabbles in sin on his way back to the Puritan stronghold, he is still a Calvinist at heart. If he is to remain true to himself and honest, as Hester says he must for his conscience's sake, then he must go back to the world in which he is comfortable, even if it eventually means his public humiliation and death. He would not feel at home in the forest where the laws of nature surpass the bars that imprison individuals in Boston.

In the end Hester escapes the iron rules of Massachusetts Bay Colony, later to return of her own volition. She assures other sinners that "at some brighter period, when the world should have grown ripe for it, in Heaven's own time, a new truth would be revealed, in order to establish the whole relation between man and woman on a surer ground of mutual happiness." This is Hawthorne's way of saying that this stern and joyless society will eventually move more toward the laws of nature as a basis for public and private behavior. By the end of the novel, his sympathies lie with Hester as a prophetess of a better time and place where personal relationships can be based on more compassionate beliefs.

In choosing Puritan New England as his backdrop, Hawthorne has provided a rich texture for his drama of human suffering. His ending, written in the nineteenth century, seems a hopeful sign that future generations will move toward a less gloomy, less repressive society where human compassion and tolerance will balance the community laws.

The Scarlet Letter as a Gothic Romance

Hawthorne is chiefly remembered as the creative genius who sought to define the romance. He contributed four major romances to the world's literature: *The House of the Seven Gables, The Blithedale Romance, The Marble Faun,* and *The Scarlet Letter.* In each of these he sought, in the prefaces, to define what romance meant to him. In the Custom House preface of *The Scarlet Letter,* Hawthorne discusses part of his concept or definition of the romance novel. He explains that life seen through moonlight is the subject of the novel. If the writer is sitting in a room in the moonlight and looks around at the familiar items on the floor—a wicker carriage or a hobby horse, for example—he can discern a quality of "strangeness and remoteness" in these familiar objects. And so he has found a territory in which the familiar becomes enchanted and "the floor of our familiar room has become a neutral territory, somewhere between the real world and fairy-land, where the Actual and the Imaginary may meet, and each imbue itself with the nature of the other." Hawthorne believes that " . . . at such an hour, and with this scene before him, if a man, sitting all lone, cannot dream strange things, and make them look like truth, he need never try to write romances."

Finally, *The Scarlet Letter* is a *psychological* romance. Hawthorne proposes to study the effects of sin on the lives of his characters. Far ahead of his time, he delves into human alienation and what it does to the soul. Doubt and self-torture provide psychological shadows in the character of Dimmesdale. Rebellion and defiance in the face of repressive laws can be seen in his heroine, Hester Prynne. She may be forced to wear the scarlet letter, but she mocks that sentence with her elaborate embroidery. The Puritan concern with man's depravity and its effect on individual characters is intertwined throughout the plot. What happens when a person has an excess of passion or intellect? When a balance of the two is not achieved in an individual, what is the end result? Within the framework of the romance, Hawthorne lays out his evidence of the psychological conflicts within and around his characters.

The Real and the Imaginary

What this means for the modern reader of *The Scarlet Letter* is that, even though Hawthorne's story has a historical setting—Boston in the 1640s—the story includes elements that are not realistic. While the Puritan society was real and can be researched, the tale also contains elements of that society that are colored by marvelous imagination in his novel.

Does this mean that there will be no limits to what Hawthorne can manufacture in his fancy? No, there are restraints. Hawthorne attempted to explain those conventions in his preface to *The House of the Seven Gables*, his next novel:

"When a writer calls his work a romance, it need hardly be observed that he wishes to claim certain latitude, both as to its fashion and material, which he would not have felt himself entitled to assume had he professed to be writing a novel. The latter form of composition is presumed to aim at a very minute fidelity, not merely to the possible, but to the probably and ordinary course of man's experience. The former—

while, as a work of art, it must rigidly subject itself to laws, and while it sins unpardonably so far as it may swerve aside from the truth of the human heart—has fairly a right to present that truth under circumstances, to a great extent, of the writer's own choosing or creation. If he think fit, also, he may so manage his atmospherical medium as to bring out or mellow the lights and deepen and enrich the shadows of the picture. He will be wise, no doubt, to make very moderate use of the privileges here stated, and, especially, to mingle the Marvellous rather as a slight, delicate, and evanescent flavor, than as any portion of the actual substance of the dish offered to the public."

Thus, the romance can have the imaginary, the supernatural, and the unbelievable, but it must also have events that do not swerve from what the human heart knows to be true. The setting of Boston in the 1640s is a perfect choice for this type of writing. Seventeenth century Bostonians believed in devils, witches, and a vengeful and angry God. So not only is Hawthorne truthful to present his setting in that light, but he also leaves ample room for the imagined and the extraordinary.

Romances can concern real settings but are not limited to the probable. The fantastic can be added, and, in *The Scarlet Letter*, Hawthorne adds the scarlet *A* in the sky at midnight, the same letter allegedly carved into Dimmesdale's breast, the sunlight that follows Pearl but not her mother, and Chillingworth descending into hell. But there must be a balance; the probable must outweigh the strange and improbable, which leads to another tenet of Hawthorne's romance definition.

Unity and Structure

Certain artistic laws must be faithfully executed so that the reader can follow the trail. There must be unity and structure, literary devices, and a subject kept ever in the reader's sight. In *The Scarlet Letter*, the scaffold scenes provide the unity and structure, and the literary devices include symbols, colors of light and darkness, irony, and the consistent subject of guilt to provide artistic wholeness. While Hawthorne can go beyond the probable and use the marvelous, he must also do so without chaos; hence, he must provide artistic balance.

Gothic Elements

These definitions of Hawthorne's romance are also joined by another tradition: Gothic elements. Gothic novels often featured supernatural events, gloomy atmospheres, castles, and the mysterious. While eighteenth century writers did not like these subjects, the Romantic authors of the nineteenth century and their successors did. Edgar Allan Poe, William Faulkner, and Stephen King all have elements of the Gothic in their stories.

Traditionally, there are a number of these Gothic elements. One used by romantic authors is a manuscript that is purported to be the origin of the story. In The Custom House preface, Hawthorne finds such a manuscript left by Surveyor Pue and a scarlet letter that is a magical artifact intertwining the real and the imaginary.

Besides magic, often Gothic stories have castles; in *The Scarlet Letter,* Governor Bellingham's home serves this purpose. It is covered with cabalistic figures and diagrams and has turrets like a castle. Inside is a set of armor, also a familiar element of the Gothic. In this armor which acts as a mirror, Pearl sees the distorted scarlet letter.

A crime, often illicit love, is usually the subject of a Gothic novel. Hester's affair is the crime committed in the Puritan community. Gothic novels sometimes have a villain who is identified as the evil person by some deformity. Chillingworth has such a deformed shoulder. And, finally, nature is often used to set the atmosphere of the story and provide some of the symbols. Nature abounds in *The Scarlet Letter,* and darkness, shadows and moonlight are all part of the Gothic ambience. The overall atmosphere of the novel is dark and gloomy, a proper milieu for the Gothic tradition.

In writing *The Scarlet Letter,* Hawthorne was striking out in a new direction, the psychological romance, while using some of the elements of a far older tradition, the Gothic novel. Modern readers should not be surprised to find horrifying revelations, sinister red light coming from a character's eyes, a precocious child who is a living symbol rather than a human being, and the dark recesses of the human heart and conscience. These elements have kept readers enthralled for generations.

The Structure of *The Scarlet Letter*

While many critics have imposed various structures on this novel, the scaffold scenes are by far the most popular means of pointing out the perfect balance of Hawthorne's masterpiece. These scenes unite the plot, themes, and symbols in a perfect balance.

The First Scaffold Scene

The first scaffold scene, which occurs in Chapters 1–3, focuses on Hester and the scarlet letter. She stands on the scaffold with quiet defiance, holding her baby in her arms. Meanwhile, a crowd of townspeople has gathered to watch her humiliation and hear a sermon. Her husband, Roger Chillingworth, has just returned and is in the outskirts of the crowd. Her lover, Arthur Dimmesdale, shares her platform but not her public humiliation.

The principal characters are all here. The townspeople are present to pass judgement, just as they will be in the final scaffold scene. Hester stands alone with Pearl in her arms, a mere infant and sign of her sin. Dimmesdale, with other officials who represent the church-state, shares the platform. His ambivalence about maintaining his silence can be seen in his demand that Hester tell the name of the child's father. In the crowd is also Roger Chillingworth whose voice is added to those of the crowd when demanding that Hester reveal her partner in sin. In this scene, we have Hester's public repentance, Dimmesdale's reluctance to admit his own guilt, and the beginning of Chillingworth's fiendish plot to find and punish the father. The focus on the adultery and the letter is strengthened by the topic of sin in Mr. Wilson's sermon.

The Second Scaffold Scene

The second scaffold scene again provides a view of all the principal characters, a dramatic vision of the scarlet *A*, and one of the most memorable tableaus in American literature. In the covering of darkness, Dimmesdale has made his way to the scaffold to perform a silent vigil of his own. So far we have seen Dimmesdale's conscious attempt to deal with his guilt, but now we go deep into his subconscious. In his spiritual torture, he cries out with a shriek of agony that is heard by Hester and Pearl as they journey to their home from the bed of the dying Governor Winthrop. This cry is also heard by Mr. Wilson.

Hester and Pearl join Dimmesdale on the scaffold, the place where seven long years earlier "Hester Prynne had lived through her first hours of public ignominy." Although the crowd is gone, Pearl asks the minister if he will join her and Hester there at noontide. He replies that their meeting will be instead at the great judgement day rather than here in the daylight. As though to taunt him, a great meteor burns through the dark sky, illuminating the scaffold, the street, and the houses. Hawthorne describes the scene as "an electric chain," the minister and his lover holding hands with their child between them. Also illuminated in the darkness is the fiendish face of Roger Chillingworth. This time, although the townspeople are not present, they talk about the scarlet *A* in the sky throughout the next day.

The chapter abounds in symbols: the scaffold itself; Dimmesdale's standing on it; the three potential observers representing Church, State, and the World of Evil; the "electric chain" of Hester, Pearl, and Dimmesdale; Pearl's appeal to Dimmesdale to stand with them; the revealing light from the heavens; and the variation on the letter *A*.

The Third Scaffold Scene

The final scaffold scene occurs after the procession on Election Day. In this powerful scene, Dimmesdale regains his soul, Pearl gains her humanity, Chillingworth loses his victim, and Hester loses her dreams.

Here again, the main characters come together, and this time Dimmesdale reveals his "scarlet letter." His Election Day sermon should have brought him his greatest triumph, but instead that honor is saved for his confession of sin and his final act of penance in standing on the scaffold with his lover and child. He escapes the diabolical clutches of Chillingworth who, without his victim, shrivels and dies. But he also triumphs over the evil that has overwhelmed him as he publicly confesses his part in Pearl's birth. He has learned that happiness must be willed not by himself, but by God. In this final scaffold scene, all the symbols and characters are once again present: the Church and State, the world of evil, the scarlet letter, the punishing scaffold, and a symbolic kiss. And, of course, death is present also.

CliffsNotes Review

Use this CliffsNotes Review to test your understanding of the original text and reinforce what you've learned in this book. After you work through the review and essay questions, identify the quote section, and the fun and useful practice projects, you're well on your way to understanding a comprehensive and meaningful interpretation of *The Scarlet Letter*.

Q&A

1. By punishing Hester with the scarlet letter, the Puritan community is
   a. being reasonable about their justice
   b. following the principles of religious forgiveness
   c. proclaiming its own smug self-righteousness

2. Two symbolic images of the good and evil battling over Dimmesdale's soul are
   a. Pearl and Hester
   b. Chillingworth and Pearl
   c. Chillingworth and Mistress Hibbins

3. As time goes by, Hester's scarlet letter comes to stand for
   a. amends
   b. articulate
   c. able

4. Chillingworth became the greatest sinner in violating the human heart because
   a. he felt the church should have avenged him
   b. he single-mindedly was bent on personal revenge
   c. he neglected his young wife

5. Hester tells Dimmesdale in the forest that humans have a right to be happy and that
   a. the love she shared with him was sacred
   b. prayer could bring about their atonement
   c. the Puritan community had no right to tell them what to do

Answers: (1) c. (2) b. (3) c. (4) b. (5) a.

Identify the Quote

1. It may serve, let us hope, to symbolize some sweet moral blossom, that may be found along the track, or relieve the darkening close of a tale of human frailty and sorrow.

2. It irks me, nevertheless, that the partner of her iniquity should not, at least, stand on the scaffold by her side. But he will be known!—he will be known!—he will be known!

3. No man, for any considerable period, can wear one face to himself, and another to the multitude, without finally getting bewildered as to which may be true.

4. God gave me the child! . . .. She is my happiness!—she is my torture, none the less! . . .. Ye shall not take her! I will die first!

5. What we did had a consecration of its own. We felt it so! We said so to each other! Hast thou forgotten it?

Answers: (1) [The author is speaking to the readers. He is setting the mood for his story and explaining that, despite the gloom and darkness of the tale, he has given the readers a "blossom" or positive message from his story.] (2) [Chillingworth is speaking to members of the Puritan crowd watching Hester's punishment; here he is vowing to seek revenge against her partner, a decision that puts him in league with the devil and eventually destroys him.] (3) [The author is speaking directly to the reader; this quotation defines Dimmesdale's dilemma or inner conflict over his inability to publicaly reveal his sin.] (4) [Hester is speaking to Governor Bellingham, Dimmesdale, and Chillingworth; here she defines Pearl as a symbol, explaining that she is Hester's means of punishment and redemption.] (5) [Hester is speaking to Dimmesdale in the forest; she is not penitent about their tryst. Instead, she passionately reminds the minister that they cared for each other and found a human love that was more sacred and holy than the Puritan laws.]

Essay Questions

1. Justify Hawthorne's including The Custom House preface as part of the novel.

2. Discuss how Hawthorne uses the setting in Chapter 1 to set the mood for his story.

3. Discuss the function of the following minor characters: Mistress Hibbins, Governor Bellingham, and Mr. Wilson.

4. Explain the evolving or static nature of one of the main characters.

5. Justify the use of the last chapter, "Conclusion."

6. Discuss the conflict between the Puritan law and the laws of nature or human law.

7. Explain the significance of the three scaffold scenes.

8. Using Hawthorne's symbols, demonstrate how they change in the context of the novel.

9. How do their reactions to sin make significant contributions to the changes and futures of the main characters?

Practice Projects

1. Rewrite the scene in the forest between Dimmesdale and Hester, using modern language in their dialogue.

2. Write a description of Pearl's future after the novel ends. Does she marry? Have a family? What is her life like? Be sure your choices are consistent with what you know about Pearl and the events at the end of the novel.

3. Write a short story in which you consider how *The Scarlet Letter* would have been different if Chillingworth's ship had wrecked and he had never come ashore in the New World.

4. Create a Web site for *The Scarlet Letter* with principle areas including the authors's background, as well as the setting, characters, symbols, and themes of the novel.

5. Create a collage that shows the relationships of the characters in the story and explain your thinking to your audience.

6. Act out a key scene in the story and convey the importance of its nature in the context of the book.

7. Write a report on the actual events of history in Boston during the years 1630–1650.

8. Research Hawthorne's earlier stories (described in the introduction) and explain their connection to *The Scarlet Letter*. Also included could be "The Maypole of Merrimount."

9. Research any of the following topics: Anne Hutchinson, John Winthrop, New England witchcraft/Salem, Hawthorne's Puritan ancestors, Ann Hibbins, Cotton Mather, "The Crucible."

CliffsNotes Resource Center

The learning doesn't need to stop here. CliffsNotes Resource Center shows you the best of the best—links to the best information in print and online about the author and/or related works. And don't think that this is all we've prepared for you; we've put all kinds of pertinent information at www.cliffsnotes.com. Look for all the terrific resources at your favorite bookstore or local library and on the Internet. When you're online, make your first stop www.cliffsnotes.com where you'll find more incredibly useful information about *The Scarlet Letter*.

Books

This CliffsNotes book provides a meaningful interpretation of *The Scarlet Letter*, published by Hungry Minds, Inc. If you are looking for information about the author and/or related works, check out these other publications:

The Scarlet Letter, John C. Gerber, ed., discusses in detail Hawthorne's sources, Puritanism, structure, symbols and interpretations. Part of the Twentieth Century Interpretations Series. Englewood Cliffs, NJ: Prentice-Hall Inc., 1968.

Nathaniel Hawthorne, by Terence Martin, discusses Hawthorne's symbols and allegory. New York: Twayne, 1965.

Nathaniel Hawthorne in His Times, by James R. Mellow, is a non-chronological biography that traces the influences on Hawthorne's thinking and writing. Baltimore, MD: The John Hopkins University Press, 1998.

The New England Mind: From Colony to Province, by Perry Miller, is an excellent source of information about the colonial period, Puritans, literature *and* intellectual life. Cambridge, MA: Harvard University Press, 1953.

Nathaniel Hawthorne, by Mark Van Doren, discusses the characters, conflicts, and structure of the novel. New York: William Sloane, 1957.

The American Novel and Its Tradition, by Richard Chase, describes the various critical approaches to *The Scarlet Letter*. Garden City, NY: Doubleday, 1957.

It's easy to find books published by Hungry Minds, Inc. You'll find them in your favorite bookstores (on the Internet and at a store near you). We also have three Web sites that you can use to read about all the books we publish:

- `www.cliffsnotes.com`
- `www.dummies.com`
- `www.Hungryminds.com`

Internet

Check out these Web resources for more information about Nathaniel Hawthorne and The Scarlet Letter:

Nathaniel Hawthorne Home Page at Eldritch Press, `http://eldred.ne.mediaone.net/nh/hawthorne.html`—Complete HTML texts with glossaries and notes; passages from Hawthorne's American Notebooks, biography of Hawthorne with time line and dates; criticism, helpful resources for teachers from The Discovery Channel, and links to other sites. Also, *The Scarlet Letter* text has color illustrations.

Literary Movements Page, `http://www.gonzaga.edu/faculty/campbell/enl311/litfram.html`—Information on American literary movements, particularly Puritanism in New England, romance and the novel, Salem witch trials and transcendentalism. Also there is a biography of Hawthorne, links, and a list of his works.

The Salem Home Page, `http://www.salemweb.com/`—A tour of Salem, architecture, and a great deal of information on the witch-craft trials and the museum and memorial.

The American Literary Classics Library Page, `http://www.americanliterature.com/SL/SLINDX.HTML`—The complete text of *The Scarlet Letter.*

Next time you're on the Internet, don't forget to drop by `www.cliffsnotes.com`. We created an online Resource Center that you can use today, tomorrow, and beyond.

Magazines and Journals

See these resources for more information about *The Scarlet Letter:*

Barna, Mark Richard. "Nathaniel Hawthorne and the Unpardonable Sin." *The World and I,* 1998: 324-332. Discusses Hawthorne's Puritan influences and his attitude toward those tendencies.

Bush, Harold K., Jr. "Reinventing the Puritan Fathers: George Bancroft, Nathaniel Hawthorne and the Birth of Endicott's Ghost." *American Transcendental Quarterly,* 1995: 131-152. Hawthorne's support for open dialogue among people as the democratic basis of American society.

Daniel, Janice B. "Apples of the Thoughts and Fancies: Nature as Narrator in The Scarlet Letter." *American Transcendental Quarterly,* 1993: 307+. This article contains a discussion of Hawthorne's use of nature and figurative language.

Dunne, Michael. "The Scarlet Letter on Film: Ninety Years of Revisioning." *Literature/Film Quarterly,* 1997: 30-39. Discusses all of the cinematic treatments of the novel.

Stone, Deborah A. "Sex, Lies and *The Scarlet Letter.*" *The American Prospect* 1995: 105+. Contrasts how illegitimate births are handled today compared with the stigma described in Hawthorne's novel.

Video

The Scarlet Letter. Dir. Rick Hauser. Perf. Meg Foster, John Heard, Kevin Conway. WGBH Boston Video, 1979. A four-hour, two-tape movie that originally appeared on PBS. To order this video, call WGBH Boston Video (1-800-949-8670) or write to WGBH Boston Video, POB 2284, S. Burlington, VT 05407. $29.95 plus shipping and handling.

Send Us Your Favorite Tips

In your quest for learning, have you ever experienced that sublime moment when you figure out a trick that saves time or trouble? Perhaps you realized you were taking ten steps to accomplish something that could have taken two. Or you found a little-known workaround that gets great results. If you've discovered a useful tip that helped you understand *The Scarlet Letter* and you'd like to share it, the CliffsNotes staff would love to hear from you. Go to our Web site at www. cliffsnotes.com and click the Talk to Us button. If we select your tip, we may publish it as part of CliffsNotes Daily, our exciting, free e-mail newsletter. To find out more or to subscribe to a newsletter, go to on the Web.

INDEX

A

Abnakis, 26
alchemy, 26
Alcott, Bronson, 4, 5
allegory, 43, 91
anathemas, 31
anemones, 60
Antinomian, 21
Apostle Eliot, 55
apotheosized, 73
appellation, 39
apple-peru, 18
aqua-vitae, 67
aristocracy, 70
asperity, 53
author. *See* Hawthorne, Nathaniel
autobiography, Hawthorne's, 14

B

Bacon, 34
Barna, Mark, 114
battle-axes, 24
beadle, 21
Bellingham, Governor
 described, 11, 24, 101
 mansion, 33, 98, 105
 Pearl's guardianship, 9, 32, 35, 79, 87
 symbolism, 91, 99
Bible
 glossary entries, 37, 40, 43
 images, 23
 Puritans' view, 8, 99
Black Man
 defined, 26
 Dimmesdale's guilt, 55, 63, 82
 Hester's reference, 36
 nature, 96, 100
 Pearl's view, 42, 54, 94
 Puritans' view, 86
Blithedale Romance, The, 3, 5, 102
body, soul connection, 43
books
 author's other, 3–5
 Black Man's, 100
 education, 52, 78, 84
 glossary entries, 53
 Hawthorne's influences, 2
 religious, 37
 resources, 112–114
Boston. *See also* Puritans
 glossary entries, 55, 65
 Hester's decision to stay, 27
 Puritan history, 81, 83, 97
 setting, 103–104
 synonyms, 40

Bowdoin College, 2
Bridge, Horatio, 2
Bristol, 65
Brook Farm Community, 3
buckramed, 65
Bush, Harold K., 114

C

cabalistic figures, 34
Calvin, John, 99
Caribbean, 65
catechism, 9, 35–36
characters. *See also* characters by name
 Hawthorne's focus, 8
 list, 11
 symbolism, 36, 42–43, 83–84, 91–94
Chase, Rober,t 112
children's literature, 5
Chillingworth, Roger
 character analysis, 83, 85
 described, 11, 19
 Dimmesdale's escape, 71, 73, 107
 Dimmesdale's torture, 44–45, 56, 64, 107
 fate, 74, 75, 80
 Hester's defiance, 79, 80
 lovers' escape plans, 66, 67, 70, 87, 102
 Pearl's view, 46
 scholarship, pursuit of, 25
 search for Pearl's father, 38–43
 symbolism, 23, 47, 95, 100, 104
 transformation, 36, 51, 52
Christmas plays, 37
Chronicles of England, 34
Church of England, 98
church officer, 43
church-state link, 99–100
clergy, 98
CliffsNotes Resource Center, 112,–114
CliffsNotes Review, 109–111
cloak, 48
clothing
 Chillingworth, 83
 glossary entries, 21, 70
 Hester's for Puritans, 28
 Hester's transformation, 61
 Pearl, 30, 32–33, 87–88
 Puritan, 16, 95, 96, 98
 Puritan laws, 29
 scarlet letter, 20, 94
Coke, 34
collar, 21, 70
College of Arms, 70
color, 95, 96
columbines, 60
commodiousness, 40
commoners, 29, 67
conscience, 88, 89
cope, 48
Cornwall, 67

CliffsNotes

LITERATURE NOTES

Absalom, Absalom!
The Aeneid
Agamemnon
Alice in Wonderland
All the King's Men
All the Pretty Horses
All Quiet on the
  Western Front
All's Well &
  Merry Wives
American Poets of the
  20th Century
American Tragedy
Animal Farm
Anna Karenina
Anthem
Antony and Cleopatra
Aristotle's Ethics
As I Lay Dying
The Assistant
As You Like It
Atlas Shrugged
Autobiography of
  Ben Franklin
Autobiography of
  Malcolm X
The Awakening
Babbit
Bartleby & Benito
  Cereno
The Bean Trees
The Bear
The Bell Jar
Beloved
Beowulf
The Bible
Billy Budd & Typee
Black Boy
Black Like Me
Bleak House
Bless Me, Ultima
The Bluest Eye & Sula
Brave New World
Brothers Karamazov

The Call of the Wild &
  White Fang
Candide
The Canterbury Tales
Catch-22
Catcher in the Rye
The Chosen
The Color Purple
Comedy of Errors...
Connecticut Yankee
The Contender
The Count of
  Monte Cristo
Crime and Punishment
The Crucible
Cry, the Beloved
  Country
Cyrano de Bergerac
Daisy Miller &
  Turn...Screw
David Copperfield
Death of a Salesman
The Deerslayer
Diary of Anne Frank
Divine Comedy-I.
  Inferno
Divine Comedy-II.
  Purgatorio
Divine Comedy-III.
  Paradiso
Doctor Faustus
Dr. Jekyll and Mr. Hyde
Don Juan
Don Quixote
Dracula
Electra & Medea
Emerson's Essays
Emily Dickinson Poems
Emma
Ethan Frome
The Faerie Queene
Fahrenheit 451
Far from the Madding
  Crowd
A Farewell to Arms
Farewell to Manzanar
Fathers and Sons
Faulkner's Short Stories

Faust Pt. I & Pt. II
The Federalist
Flowers for Algernon
For Whom the Bell Tolls
The Fountainhead
Frankenstein
The French
  Lieutenant's Woman
The Giver
Glass Menagerie &
  Streetcar
Go Down, Moses
The Good Earth
The Grapes of Wrath
Great Expectations
The Great Gatsby
Greek Classics
Gulliver's Travels
Hamlet
The Handmaid's Tale
Hard Times
Heart of Darkness &
  Secret Sharer
Hemingway's
  Short Stories
Henry IV Part 1
Henry IV Part 2
Henry V
House Made of Dawn
The House of the
  Seven Gables
Huckleberry Finn
I Know Why the
  Caged Bird Sings
Ibsen's Plays I
Ibsen's Plays II
The Idiot
Idylls of the King
The Iliad
Incidents in the Life of
  a Slave Girl
Inherit the Wind
Invisible Man
Ivanhoe
Jane Eyre
Joseph Andrews
The Joy Luck Club
Jude the Obscure

Julius Caesar
The Jungle
Kafka's Short Stories
Keats & Shelley
The Killer Angels
King Lear
The Kitchen God's Wife
The Last of the
  Mohicans
Le Morte d'Arthur
Leaves of Grass
Les Miserables
A Lesson Before Dying
Light in August
The Light in the Forest
Lord Jim
Lord of the Flies
The Lord of the Rings
Lost Horizon
Lysistrata & Other
  Comedies
Macbeth
Madame Bovary
Main Street
The Mayor of
  Casterbridge
Measure for Measure
The Merchant
  of Venice
Middlemarch
A Midsummer Night's
  Dream
The Mill on the Floss
Moby-Dick
Moll Flanders
Mrs. Dalloway
Much Ado About
  Nothing
My Ántonia
Mythology
Narr. ...Frederick
  Douglass
Native Son
New Testament
Night
1984
Notes from the
  Underground

___

Check Out the All-New CliffsNotes Guides

TECHNOLOGY TOPICS

PERSONAL FINANCE TOPIC

CAREER TOPICS